WHEN
EVIL
STOPS HIDING

By Martin Mawyer
Christian Action Network

When Evil Stops Hiding
Inside the Kingdom of the Beast

By Martin Mawyer

ISBN #: 978-0-9850267-2-1

Interior Design and Layout: Patti A. Pierucci

TABLE OF CONTENTS

PROLOGUE

'The Devil's Not Hiding."

If this were fiction, you'd dismiss it as too far-fetched.

A neo-Nazi Satanist who preaches child sacrifice and ritual murder—secretly working for the FBI?

A government informant who gets paid to run a death cult—while his writings inspire real-world killings, terror plots, and the grooming of children online?

That's not a thriller. It's a bad screenplay—one that never should have made it past the first draft.

And yet ... it happened.

This is not a conspiracy theory. This is not a whispered rumor. The names are real. The court documents are real. The dead are real.

The informant's name is Joshua Caleb Sutter.

And while collecting government paychecks, he was also publishing books that glorified torture, rape, infanticide, and cannibalism in the name of "Satanic enlightenment."

These weren't obscure rants shared in some edgy book club. They were used by terrorist groups like **Atomwaffen Division** to recruit, radicalize, and justify bloodshed. They were adopted by online cells like **764** to terrorize children into producing self-harm videos and explicit content.

And the FBI knew. They paid him anyway.

You could stop reading here. Shut the book. Tell yourself it's all conspiracy nonsense. Go back to the easier world where the bad guys are dumb, obvious, and far away.

But the real enemy is smarter than that. He doesn't wear horns. He wears a suit. A robe. A badge. Sometimes ... all three.

This book isn't about fearmongering. It's about understanding what happens when belief becomes a weapon, and institutions choose chaos over truth. When evil stops hiding—not because it's brave, but because it's protected.

You're not crazy for wanting to deny it.

But you'll want to keep reading anyway.

These groups don't offer policy. They offer collapse.

They have no vision of what comes after the destruction they so eagerly seek. No philosophy, no structure, no moral code. Just the promise of power through chaos.

And that's the signature of Satan.

Throughout history, his servants have never been builders. They are destroyers. They seduce the disillusioned with whispers of revolution, initiation, and hidden knowledge. They convince the wounded and the angry that tearing everything down will lead to freedom. That they will be the ones to rise from the ruins, crowned in fire and glory.

But the truth is this: They don't know what they're building— because they're not meant to.

Satan never shows his blueprint. He doesn't need to. He only needs obedience, outrage, and a willingness to burn down the world without asking what replaces it.

And that is what we are witnessing now.

A generation of the deceived is being groomed not just to reject goodness, but to annihilate it to make the world desperate enough, confused enough, and broken enough to welcome anything that promises order—even if it drips with blood.

They are not the architects. They are the demolition crew.

And when the smoke clears, something will step forward to take the throne.

Not because it was earned.

But because it was prepared for him.

All of this—every cult, every ideology, every ritualized perversion—is building a kingdom. Not randomly—and certainly not metaphorically. It is being prepared. But a throne for whom? The **Antichrist**?

Read on, and draw your own conclusions. But you'll see—the Devil is not even trying to hide in sheep's clothing.

Note to Readers:

This book includes terminology, references, and names that may be unfamiliar—some pulled from dark-web subcultures, criminal investigations, or extremist ideologies. If you encounter a term in bold lettering that you don't recognize or need to recall, please consult the glossary at the end of this book. You've already seen a few in this prologue. You're not expected to know every term at first glance. That's why the glossary exists—so truth doesn't get buried in confusion.

CHAPTER 1

THE DIGITAL ABYSS OF BRADLEY CADENHEAD

You'd never guess it by looking at the church bulletin, but somewhere in the pews of Washington Street Baptist sat the boy who would become one of America's most reviled online predators.

Bradley Chance Cadenhead wasn't born evil. He was baptized, bullied, and broken. A child of divorce, depression, and digital immersion, he began life in Stephenville, Texas, as a quiet, God-fearing kid.

But by age fifteen, holed up in a dim bedroom strewn with electronics and rot, he had become "Felix"—the self-proclaimed CP (child predator) god, the founder of **764**, a virtual cult of sadists who groomed children, mutilated pets, traded in human degradation, and laughed at law enforcement.

By age nineteen, Cadenhead wasn't just another statistic of mental illness or system failure. He was the reason the FBI now classifies groups like **764** as domestic terror threats.

Cadenhead's transformation was slow and mostly invisible to the adults in his life. His mother began drinking and leaving home when he was just ten. In middle school, the bullying started. Classmates described him as an "easy target," shy and awkward, often whispering to himself.

5

Bradley Cadenhead

When his parents split in 2016, Cadenhead began a steady slide into isolation and psychological distress. He dropped out of school at age fifteen and retreated into the online world, where no one mocked him, and no one questioned his authority. In statements to probation officers, he said simply, "I stopped caring about everything."

From his bedroom, he discovered **Discord**—a chat platform originally designed for gamers. There, he built a persona around sadism, control, and digital cruelty. He adopted the name "Felix" and founded a server called **764**, named after part of his Texas zip code.

Through it, he attracted predators and victims from around the world. He used child pornography not out of sexual compulsion, he later told authorities, but as a tool—to lure abusers, groom children, and force his followers to submit.

The tactics were monstrous.

Cadenhead extorted nude images from minors, then blackmailed them into harming themselves or their pets on camera. He demanded they carve messages onto their bodies and forced them to degrade themselves for the amusement of his growing cult of followers.

In several instances, young users were coerced into acts of animal cruelty, including the decapitation of hamsters, to prove loyalty. He manipulated depressed teens, sometimes encouraging them to kill themselves, and bragged online about how law enforcement was powerless to stop him.

And for a long time, he was right.

Discord shut down his accounts only after repeated reports. Each time, he reappeared under new aliases. By the time police traced the abuse back to his mother's apartment in Stephenville, Cadenhead had created more than 400 **Discord** profiles. He taunted users with messages like "Felix the CP god" and sneered at the FBI, claiming he'd been reported dozens of times without consequence.

By the time police traced the abuse back to his mother's apartment in Stephenville, Cadenhead's bedroom had become a dark lair of digital abuse. In August 2021, law enforcement executed a search warrant and found the room reeking, cluttered with electronics, and a laptop containing illegal images and videos.

Among the content was a video of a man smoking heroin in Cadenhead's honor, messages from teens who had self-harmed at his instruction, and clips of minors carving "I ♥ CP764" into their skin.

At his sentencing, prosecutor Jett Smith put it plainly: "Very rarely do we get a chance to look evil in the face. This may be one of those times."

Despite being only nineteen years old, Cadenhead was given 80 years in prison—a punishment typically reserved for serial offenders or violent criminals. But the judge, after reviewing the evidence, invoked the Bible's seven deadly sins. "There is something horribly wrong with you," he told Cadenhead. "Horribly."

Some of those who knew him in real life couldn't reconcile the boy they remembered with the monster the world now saw. A former Bible study teacher recalled young Bradley accepting Christ. A classmate remembered him curled up on the floor, sobbing and babbling. Friends recalled the quiet kid who never fought back.

But online, among the twisted corners of **Discord** and **Telegram**, Cadenhead was a god. He was the founder of a digital cult that lives on, even after his arrest. In April 2022, long after he was locked away, a user in a **764**-affiliated server posted, "We would be **764** gods if Brad was here."

The reach of **764** didn't end with him. New cells began emerging globally, with offshoots like **764 Inferno** operating in Greece and North Carolina. Their tactics mimicked Cadenhead's playbook—psychological torture, self-harm challenges, and glorification of gore and domination. Arrests in multiple countries, including Canada, exposed how the ideology had metastasized.

The FBI now considers **764** a domestic terror threat, with investigations open in all 56 field offices. Cyber tipline reports related to the group surged by more than 200 percent in just one year. Its loose, decentralized structure mimics the **Order of Nine Angles** (see Chapter 3), with which it shares disturbing ideological overlaps—including ritualized dehumanization, glorification of suffering, and contempt for conventional morality.

And that is the terror of the new age: Evil doesn't die when the body is caged. It lives in networks, in usernames, in screenshots passed from one disturbed child to another. It evolves, splinters, and rebrands. It survives on the belief that no one will take it seriously, because who could believe a teenager from a Texas church pew could mastermind an international ring of digital sadists?

But it happened.

And this is just the beginning.

CHAPTER 2

THE TEMPEL OV BLOOD

If there's a face behind the digital cults spreading bloodlust and chaos in the name of Satanic enlightenment, it belongs to Joshua Caleb Sutter. He's not just a provocateur. He's the founder of the **Tempel ov Blood**—one of the most disturbing nexions of occult extremism ever to operate online. His story is a case study in how radical ideologies fester in the shadows of the internet, and how one man turned cruelty into currency, all while getting paid by the U.S. government.

Raised in a conservative household, Sutter veered hard in the opposite direction. He immersed himself in occultism, drew from the neo-Nazi mythos, and built a theology rooted in ritualistic violence and moral inversion. The result was the **Tempel ov Blood**—a secretive order preaching that true spiritual evolution can only be achieved by embracing one's darkest impulses: pain, degradation, and destruction.

It wasn't metaphorical. It was operational.

The group's name is no exaggeration. They glorify blood rituals, psychological torture, and sexual transgression. Sutter's writings urge followers to break every societal taboo—to reject empathy, morality, and conscience. In his view, the path to transcendence runs through total depravity. And tragically, others listened.

To understand his message, one must understand **Aeonic**

9

Evolution—the belief that history unfolds through violent cycles and that the current age must be destroyed so a new, superior **Aeon** can rise. For Sutter, that meant accelerating collapse through spiritual subversion, institutional infiltration, and ritualized harm. His writings helped turn that theory into practice—online, offline, and everywhere the vulnerable could be reached.

Joshua Caleb Sutter

What makes Sutter's story truly shocking is his longtime role as a paid FBI informant. For years, he provided intelligence to federal authorities while simultaneously publishing texts that glorified rape, child sacrifice, and murder. His dual identity allowed him to operate with a disturbing level of impunity, spreading ideological poison while under the protection of those sworn to stop it.

Sutter's alliance with the **Order of Nine Angles (O9A)** was no accident. **O9A**'s teachings, steeped in militant Satanism and esoteric Nazism, aligned perfectly with his aims. By linking **Tempel ov Blood** to **O9A**'s global network, Sutter found a ready audience of extremists who shared his vision of a world purified by suffering and reborn through violence. Together, they advanced the gospel of **Aeon**ic destruction.

Tempel ov Blood members were encouraged to undergo "spiritual transgressions"—rituals that often included self-mutilation, animal sacrifice, and grotesque sexual acts. These weren't symbolic practices. They were designed to

Angel Luis Almeida

harden the initiate, to burn away empathy, and to sever any remaining ties to human decency. This wasn't just about belief. It was about transformation through trauma.

The internet was Sutter's most potent weapon.

Hidden behind encrypted channels and anonymous handles, he built a digital temple of horror. He and his followers recruited disaffected youth, shared disturbing images and texts, and built a cult around domination and dehumanization. In this dark corner of cyberspace, sadism became a sacrament—and Sutter, a prophet.

His influence spread.

Groups like Bradley Cadenhead's **764** borrowed heavily from **Tempel ov Blood** doctrine, fusing online exploitation with **O9A**'s ritualistic depravity. Sutter's teachings were no longer fringe; they were metastasizing, reaching new minds in every corner of the digital world. And they were leaving victims in their wake.

Case in point: Angel Luis Almeida. A 23-year-old from New York, Almeida came under FBI scrutiny after an anonymous tip revealed his grotesque online presence, one steeped in child abuse, animal torture,

11

and explicit allegiance to the **Tempel ov Blood** (ToB). When agents raided his apartment, they found a firearm, Satanic texts, and a ToB flag. His social media celebrated pedophilia and violence, hallmarks of the cult's dehumanizing ethos.

The social media posts attributed to Almeida were nothing short of despicable. They included photos of him brandishing firearms with captions such as "For the 2K pedophile haters" and images of him wearing a T-shirt that read "kiddie fiddler" in front of a computer monitor displaying the message, "I am addicted to hardcore child pornography."

These posts underscored the group's fixation on pedophilia and sexual assault, which are central to their ideology of dehumanization and spiritual evolution through transgression.

And Almeida wasn't alone. From military infiltrators like Ethan Melze —who plotted a "mass-casualty ambush" on his fellow soldiers— to child predators lurking in private **Discord** servers, the fingerprints of **Tempel ov Blood** and **O9A** are everywhere. Their ideology isn't confined to old books. It's moving. Recruiting. Acting.

The arrest and conviction of members like Almeida and Melzer serve as grim reminders that these aren't just dangerous ideas. They're operational blueprints. They radicalize. They dehumanize. They destroy. And at the center of it all was Joshua Caleb Sutter—ruthless ideologue by night, paid federal asset by day.

This isn't irony. It's complicity. While taxpayers funded his cooperation, Sutter disseminated texts that inspired suicide, terrorism, and the sexual exploitation of children. His books turned belief into action. His rituals turned shame into status. And all the while, the taxpayer checks cleared.

To understand how this could happen—how one man could exploit the system while pushing civilization toward collapse—we have to go back. Before the gore servers. Before the livestreamed rituals. Before the nexions and cults and digital carnage. We have to go to the source.

His name is David Myatt. He didn't just spread the fire.

He lit the match.

CHAPTER 3

THE MAN BEHIND THE ORDER

David Myatt doesn't appear to be the architect of a death cult. There are no black robes. No pentagram tattoos. No Instagram selfies with blood and horns.

What he does have is far more dangerous: a long memory, a quiet tongue, and an ideology that has inspired neo-Nazi terrorists, jihadis, school shooters, child abusers, and online sadists across the globe.

For decades, Myatt moved in the margins. A drifter through extremist scenes. A Nazi one year, a Muslim the next, a Satanist always. His name rarely appeared in headlines. But his words—spread through thousands of pages of manifestos, essays, and cryptic occult writings—birthed something monstrous. Something he never had to carry out himself.

It was called the **Order of Nine Angles**.

And it may be the most evil ideology you've never heard of.

Myatt was born in 1950, raised partly in colonial Africa and partly in post-war Britain. He studied physics and philosophy. He dabbled in mysticism and joined the neo-Nazi movements in the 1960s and 1970s. Eventually, he led Britain's National Socialist Movement, a small but violent group committed to fascist revolution.

But while others were chanting in the streets, Myatt was building

David Myatt

something slower. Something deeper.

He began publishing under the pseudonym Anton Long, crafting a new theology—one that merged Hitler's racial hatred with that of Aleister Crowley's occult transgressions. The **Order of Nine Angles**, or **O9A**, was never meant for the masses. It was designed for the very few—those willing to cross every line, shed every belief, and become gods of their own cruel universes.

The writings were scattered, layered in metaphors and symbols. Some were printed in limited zines—small, non-commercial magazines. Others passed hand to hand among radicals. All carried the same theme: Morality is weakness, violence is sacred, and spiritual evolution requires blood.

Central to **O9A** is the concept of **Aeonic Evolution**—the belief that human civilizations rise and fall in great cycles, and that the current world (the age of democracy, Christianity, and traditional liberalism) must be destroyed to birth a new, higher order.

How will that be achieved?

Through transgression.

Not metaphorical transgression. Literal.

According to **O9A** texts, followers must break taboos not just to prove loyalty, but to transform themselves. Ritual murder (called "**Opfer**"), rape, child abuse, infiltration of enemies, and acts of terrorism are not crimes in their doctrine. They are tools of becoming.

To operationalize this descent into moral ruin, **O9A** created what it calls the **Seven-Fold Way**—a multi-stage initiatory system that masks spiritual rot as mystical growth. On the surface, it resembles an esoteric path of self-discipline and philosophical awakening. In practice, it's a gauntlet of psychological warfare that breaks down the human conscience.

Initiates are told to complete stages involving intense physical isolation, infiltration of societal institutions, and acts of "**culling**"—a euphemism for ritual murder. One key phase, the "**Insight Role**," demands that adherents embed themselves inside systems they claim to hate—military units, religious institutions, law enforcement—and slowly erode them from within. The goal isn't exposure. It's corruption.

This structured ambiguity—the mix of dense terminology, invented rites, and obscure symbolism—serves a purpose. Like the slang-drenched dystopia of *A Clockwork Orange*, **O9A** deliberately cloaks its evil in invented language: "**Opfer**" instead of sacrifice. "Nexion" instead of chapter. "**Aeonic Evolution**" instead of annihilation. It's not just to confuse outsiders. It's to create a linguistic wall that only the truly committed will be able to climb.

Confusion becomes a filter. Complexity becomes a test of loyalty.

Some members are assigned what's called an "**Insight Role**"—a period of six to eighteen months in which they must join a mainstream institution they wish to destroy. The military. The police. The clergy. The goal isn't espionage. It's corrosion. Rot the system from within.

David Myatt himself allegedly walked this path.

In the early 2000s, he suddenly announced his conversion to Islam, adopting the name Abdul-Aziz ibn Myatt and aligning himself with jihadist groups. He praised Osama bin Laden. Authored Islamist tracts. Preached global war against the West.

Was it sincere? Or just another mask?

He later renounced Islam and returned to "pagan mysticism" and esoteric studies. His apologists claimed this proved he had changed. His critics said it was classic **O9A** strategy: embed, learn, corrupt, retreat.

All the while, his writings—many still under the Anton Long name—continued to spread. Across obscure forums. In anarchist occult bookstores. Inside neo-Nazi groups like **Atomwaffen Division**. In the chatrooms of self-described "rape cults" like **RapeWaffen**. And eventually, into the digital torture cells of **764**.

Atomwaffen Division, founded in the United States around

2015, was a neo-Nazi **accelerationist** group obsessed with total civilizational collapse—its name translating from German as "nuclear weapons." To its members, race war, terrorism, and mass death weren't nightmares. They were goals.

Out of that nihilistic theology emerged **RapeWaffen**, a splinter cell even more depraved. Drawing directly from **O9A** texts, **RapeWaffen** didn't just embrace sexual violence—it worshiped it. Its members believed that rape, like ritual murder, could serve as a spiritual offering to higher, darker powers.

Both groups adopted the language, symbols, and ideology of the **Order of Nine Angles**. And both left victims in their wake.

These threads tie back to him.

To the man who gave Satanism a military manual.

Law enforcement has taken notice. Britain's Home Office has debated labeling **O9A** as a terrorist organization officially. The U.S. military has investigated suspected adherents in its ranks. Even NATO has issued internal alerts about **O9A** infiltration tactics.

But David Myatt? He walks free.

Now in his seventies, he lives quietly in rural England. He has denied being Anton Long. Denied founding the Order. Denied responsibility for the deaths, the assaults, the radicalization.

Always denying. Always one step removed.

And maybe that's the most dangerous part.

The Devil doesn't always deal the cards. Sometimes he just writes the rules, folds his hands, and watches what happens next.

In the next chapter, we'll see how those rules—set by Myatt decades ago—spread from the dark corners of British libraries into the devices of American teenagers. How **O9A**'s gospel of "**sacred violence**" became a digital contagion. And how a new generation is now being taught that cruelty is a kind of prayer.

Because the Order didn't vanish.

It evolved.

CHAPTER 4
THE RITUAL OF COLLAPSE

They told us it was fringe.

The **Order of Nine Angles. Tempel ov Blood. Atomwaffen Division. RapeWaffen**. Just obscure names swirling in the corners of the internet, gathering dust in intelligence files. It was easier to mock them than to study them. Easier to treat them like malformed role-playing games than what they really were:

Blueprints.

Rituals.

An architecture of destruction.

We now know these groups were never just about esoteric ideology or fringe occultism. They were laying the foundation for a new kind of war—spiritual, cultural, and psychological. A war fought not with armies, but with memes, livestreams, rituals, and sacrifice. A war without declarations. A war without uniforms. A war with one purpose: to unmake the world.

This is not chaos. This is choreography.

The Cult of Collapse

The so-called "**culling**" advocated by the **Order of Nine Angles** was never just about killing. It was about dismantling moral structures, social bonds, personal conscience. Each act of violence,

17

whether ritualistic or random, served the same dark altar. And those performing it were told they were participating in something sacred.

To them, murder is a sacrament. Betrayal is a virtue. Innocence is a currency to be spent.

This is how Satanic ideology hides behind transformation: destroy everything, promise nothing, and demand obedience. The lie is always the same—you'll be gods in the new world.

But there is no new world. Only ashes. And ashes do not build.

Ritual Without Robes

What once required secret societies and Latin chants now flows through **TikTok** filters, **Reddit** boards, and **Discord** servers. You don't need to wear a robe or chant in a forest to participate in the ritual. You only need to click "share."

The aesthetics of darkness—blood, neon pentagrams, pagan resurgence, ultraviolence, irony-laced Satanism—aren't limited to the occult underground anymore. They're woven into fashion trends, pop music, viral jokes. These aren't accidents. They're invocations.

Possession today doesn't foam at the mouth. It goes viral.

The Silence of Institutions

Law enforcement has struggled to understand these groups because they don't operate like gangs or traditional terror cells. Their crimes are often isolated. Their networks are decentralized. But their ideology is shared ... and growing.

Academia shrugs. The media yawns. Tech platforms host it, bury it, and monetize it. No one wants to call it what it is: A spiritual insurgency.

We want everything to be either political or psychological. But this is theological. Evil doesn't need to believe in itself. It only requires you not to.

These acts—the grooming of children, the infiltration of military units, the violent manifestos, the obsession with humiliation and pain—they're not just crimes.

This is a liturgy of collapse.

And the goal is not to usher in freedom. It's to break the world enough that people will accept anything. Any new order. Any new

Moral structures like churches and social bonds are being **culled**
to pave the way for the Antichrist

voice. Any leader who promises to bring peace, no matter the cost.

We are watching the altar being built. The sacrifices are being made. The language is already here. The kingdom is almost ready.

These groups aren't just destroying for destruction's sake.

They are preparing the way.

And for whom else, one might postulate, if not the **Antichrist**?

CHAPTER 5

THE GOSPEL OF ACCELERATIONISM

A ccelerationism is not just an idea. It's not just a tactic. It is, for the extremists who embrace it, a gospel—a holy mandate to burn down the world to remake it. And not in a way that restores what was lost, but in a way that clears the way for something entirely inhuman, entirely post-moral, altogether demonic.

To understand the digital cults and death-driven movements documented in the previous chapters, one must grasp the theology of destruction underlying them. Because that's what it is: a belief system that sees chaos as cleansing, violence as virtuous, and suffering as sacred.

What is Accelerationism?

In its simplest form, accelerationism is the belief that society is irreparably broken and that its collapse should not be prevented, but accelerated. This isn't merely pessimism. It's a call to action. An invocation to force the breakdown—economically, culturally, morally—so that the old order can be swept away.

In leftist versions, this seems like pushing capitalism to implode under its vulnerabilities. But in the circles that matter here—**The Com, 764, O9A**, and their ideological offspring—accelerationism is something else entirely.

21

Accelerationism sees chaos as cleansing,
violence as virtuous, and suffering as sacred

It is spiritual warfare. And the enemy is not just the government, or the elite, or the system. It is you. Your family. Your church. Your child's innocence.

The Ritual of Ruin

Accelerationism in these circles has taken on religious undertones. The more grotesque the act, the more valuable it is as an offering to this gospel of collapse. Rape, suicide, gore, mass shootings, economic sabotage—all are viewed as sacred accelerants.

The end game? Not merely to watch society fall, but to hasten its fall. And as it does, to rise in its ashes with a new order, forged by those who embraced the flames. This is how the **Galactic Imperium** (Chapter 13) becomes not just fantasy, but perceived inevitability.

These are the beliefs fueling **764**'s sadistic gamification of violence. This is why a child's suicide is rewarded with rank, why digital torture is currency. Why cutting "**764**" into the skin is a rite of passage. It isn't random cruelty. It is purposeful destruction ... ritual collapse.

From Atomwaffen to Inferno

Groups like **Atomwaffen Division**, inspired by Nazi ideology and **O9A** occultism, put this doctrine into practice. They view terror as divine. Murder as awakening. They call for racial holy war, but behind that is a broader goal: destroy the old world.

Inferno, the inner core of **764**, embraces that same logic. Members earn **Points for Pain**. Suicide is a sacrament. Custom-ordered abuse is framed as progress. The sicker the act, the higher the status. Not just for shock, but for acceleration. Every act is intended to tear the fabric of civilization one thread at a time.

It is in this culture that the idea of "collapse as creation" thrives. And it is not philosophical. It is actionable.

Accelerationism and the Antichrist

There is no clearer prophecy of accelerationism than the Book of Revelation. It describes a world engulfed in chaos, when nations are deceived, the innocent are slaughtered, and a false messiah rises from the smoke.

Accelerationism, in this spiritual context, is not a fringe political theory. It is a blueprint. A satanic sacrament. A prelude to global deception.

Those who ignite the collapse may not know whom they serve. But Scripture tells us plainly: "The dragon gave the beast his power and his throne and great authority." (Revelation 13:2)

Every act of grooming, every suicide stream, every **Lorebook** (Chapter 17) passed in digital catacombs. They are not just crimes; they are bricks in a temple of ruin—a foundation for the throne of the beast.

And yet, the Church sleeps.

The Only Gospel That Saves

The gospel of collapse must be answered with the Gospel of Christ.

Not just preached on Sunday mornings but declared with power in the face of evil. A gospel that rescues the broken, defends the vulnerable, and confronts the principalities of the digital age.

Because a collapse is coming, but only one gospel leads to resurrection. Only one cross stands taller than the towers they want to burn.

We must preach that gospel.

Before it's too late.

CHAPTER 6

THE CHILDREN ARE THE TARGET

The internet has always had its dark corners. But in **764**, those corners became catacombs—designed not for hiding, but for ritual. And the victims are not soldiers or ideological opponents. They are children.

If the **Order of Nine Angles** provided the theology, and **Tempel ov Blood** tested the liturgy, then **764** is the implementation. It is the digital death cult for a generation raised on Wi-Fi and weaponized despair.

It doesn't sell ideology. It sells pain. It doesn't preach. It provokes. It doesn't promise transformation. It demands suffering.

And that suffering has names.

The Mask Drops

Unlike its predecessors, **764** doesn't hide behind esoteric language or elaborate philosophical treatises. There are no "**seven-fold initiations**" or metaphysical essays about **Aeonic Evolution**. There is only humiliation, rape, suicide, and mutilation—streamed, shared, and encouraged across encrypted platforms.

But that absence of doctrine is not accidental. It's strategic.

764 operates without having to explain itself, because its purpose is not to argue, but to destroy. Its methods echo **O9A**'s obsession with

25

Aeonic Evolution, yet it achieves this aim without ever uttering the term. Where **O9A** cloaks its bloodshed in metaphysical jargon, **764** lets the carnage speak for itself.

O9A members who murder do not explain their reasons to the victims—and neither does **764**. Their victims are not educated, indoctrinated, or warned. They are simply used. Corrupted. Culled.

Its operators don't see themselves as cultists. They are black-masked digital executioners who treat human pain like a sport.

They don't want your political allegiance. They want your children broken.

The Known Victims

Connecticut Teen Girl—Age Seventeen

Initially targeted on **Roblox** and **Discord**, this girl was groomed into sending explicit images to her abuser. What began as online manipulation escalated into ritualistic demands, including a nude Barbie doll marked with "**764**" and a note written in her own blood. The same grooming circle persuaded her to help issue death threats to local schools.

Rosemary's Story—United Kingdom, Age Fourteen

She was a quiet teen with a fondness for anime and online forums. On **Discord**, she was invited into a private server by someone claiming to be a mentor. The "challenge" began innocently: Take a cold shower and post a photo of your arm with a red mark. But within weeks, the tasks turned violent. Self-harm, choking, and eventually cutting deeper "for the gods." On the morning she was found dead in her room, her browser was still open to the server's leaderboard. Her name had just been promoted. "**Opfer** achieved," it read.

Adrian—Ohio, Age Thirteen

A thirteen-year-old boy with no history of mental illness, no warning signs—until he started withdrawing from family, obsessively checking his phone, and staying up all night. His parents didn't know what he was watching. The **Telegram** group he joined had more than 500 members, all using cryptic terms like "**cull rank**" and "**insight tokens**." He was found dead after

Our children are the victims of the internet's dark corners, which
sells pain and corruption to the most innocent among us

what appeared to be a final "challenge." No suicide note. Only a
list of completed tasks was scrawled in a notebook.

Unnamed Girl—Internet Forum (Nickname: "KiwiFarms Opfer")

Her abuse was turned into a grotesque game. Doctored photos,
doxxing, forced degradation—broadcast in real time. The chat
logs referred to her as "**Opfer**" (human sacrifice) and exchanged
violent fantasies using phrases lifted directly from **O9A** literature.
Whether she lived or died remains unclear. What is clear: the
users didn't care. To them, she was an offering.

Kaleb Christopher Merritt Case – Virginia, USA

A member of a **764** offshoot called **CVLT**, Merritt kidnapped and raped a twelve-year-old girl. Convicted and sentenced to 350 years in prison, his case is one of the clearest judicial links between **764** and real-world predation.

Elderly Victims in Europe

In one horrifying instance, a seventeen-year-old **764** member livestreamed himself stabbing an eighty-two-year-old man and killing a seventy-four-year-old woman. The violence was not ideological. It was theatrical, a grotesque offering to the cult's perverse vision.

Jairo Jamie Tinajero—International

Pleading guilty to charges including racketeering conspiracy, **CSAM** (Child Sex Abuse Material) pos**Session**, and conspiracy to murder, Tinajero groomed minors across jurisdictions and plotted to kill one of them, revealing a far-reaching and coordinated network of abuse.

764 Inferno—Psychological Torment

Led by Leonidas Varagiannis and Prasan Nepal, this subgroup specializes in psychological torture. They order minors to carve "blood signs" into their skin and push victims into escalating acts of self-harm—all for internal status and ritual validation.

Suicide Victims – Canada & Eastern Europe

One fifteen-year-old Eastern European girl convinced a boy to livestream his own suicide. In Canada, a father lost his teenage daughter after two years of online grooming. Both cases point to **764**'s deliberate strategy: isolate, exploit, erase.

Animal Cruelty Victims

Not even animals are spared. Victims are sometimes forced to torture or kill pets as part of their "training." These acts serve as emotional desensitization, spiritual defilement, and proof of obedience.

Global Scale—FBI Investigations

The U.S. Department of Justice currently has more than 250

open investigations related to **764**. Victims have been identified across North America, Europe, and Asia. Many are under the age of thirteen.

How 764 Operates

There is no central leader. No address. No manifesto. Just a web of interconnected platforms and a shared language of brutality:
- Grooming masked as mentorship or friendship
- Dares that begin as edgy jokes and escalate into mutilation
- Ranking systems that reward harm and suicide with status
- Recorded abuse used as currency to gain access to deeper, darker channels
- They use emojis like sigils, symbolic designs. Memes as rituals. Suicide notes are sacred texts.

For those on the outside, it all looks like nonsense—until it's too late.

The Greatest Domestic Threat

This isn't jihad. It's not organized crime. These aren't school shooters. It's worse.

Because it hides behind your child's screen, it learns their vulnerabilities before you do. And it speaks in a language designed to bypass every filter, every parental control, and every moral defense.

764 doesn't just destroy lives. It turns families into crime scenes.

A Wound in the Soul of the Nation

We can argue about politics. About tech censorship. About free speech.

But none of that matters if our children are being harvested.

764 is not just a cult. It is not just a network.

It is a ritual machine, fed by the attention of the curious and the silence of the cowards.

And if we do not name it, expose it, and drive it into the light ... then the sacrifices will continue.

Because for them, every new victim is a step further in the ritual, a step further toward tearing down society, a step further toward bringing a call for a savior—an **Antichrist**?—to restore order and normality.

Whether they know it or not, they are acting as priests of pain.

And their altar is teeming with children.

CHAPTER 7

THE CONSPIRACY SMOKESCREEN

By now, the reader may be wondering: Could all this actually be true?

A network of sadists manipulating children into ritual abuse, grooming them toward suicide, creating gore-driven currency, and dreaming of a new world order called the **Galactic Imperium**? Could it really be happening—right now, in our digital backyard?

The answer is yes. Terrifyingly, documentably, yes.

And yet, that very terror is what makes the truth so vulnerable to dismissal. Not because it's untrue. But because the perpetrators have designed it that way.

One of the most effective weapons in the arsenal of digital cults, terror networks, and occult ideologues like those in **764**, **O9A**, and **The Com** isn't a computer or a cleaver. It's disinformation.

They've learned that the best way to keep people from believing the truth is to flood the world with lies that sound similar.

They poison the well.

They seed the internet with wild stories about reptilian overlords, secret Jesuit-run time machines, alien DNA conspiracies, and demonic pizza parlors—until the average person can't tell the difference between what's real and what's deliberately deranged.

It's not accidental. It's not even just for laughs. It's tactical.

The enemy knows that the best way to keep people from believing
the truth is to flood the world with lies that sound similar

Because when the public sees a headline about child torture in encrypted **Discord** rooms, or a teenager who killed himself live on a **764** channel, or an **accelerationist** group pushing for the collapse of society, they'll think: That's just more conspiracy theory garbage.

The strategy is this: bury real evil under a mountain of fake evil.

This is why it's so critical to say, as plainly as possible: Everything in this book is real.

Every case cited can be traced to news reports, arrest records, federal affidavits, or direct conversations with investigators. Every group mentioned has been referenced in law enforcement bulletins or forensic research. Every term, tactic, and ideology was chosen not to shock, but to reveal.

Because the greatest trick the Devil ever pulled wasn't just convincing the world he didn't exist; it was convincing us that anyone who did see him was crazy.

This book is not a conspiracy theory. It's an autopsy report.

And if we can't recognize the corpse for what it is, the next one might be someone we love.

CHAPTER 8

THE STRATEGY OF TENSION, FROM GLADIO TO 764

The horrors of **764** and the cults that preceded it might seem like isolated aberrations—a sick byproduct of internet anonymity and modern nihilism. But there's an older story here, one that began not in online chatrooms, but in the war rooms of post-World War II Europe.

In the late 1940s, as the Cold War froze the globe into opposing ideological camps, NATO and the CIA helped establish secret paramilitary networks across Western Europe. These were known as "stay-behind armies"—units designed to act as underground resistance fighters in the event of a Soviet invasion. Italy's version of this network would become known as **Operation Gladio**.

Its stated mission was noble. Its covert tactics were anything but.

Over the decades that followed, Gladio-affiliated operatives, particularly in Italy, became implicated in a series of terrorist attacks designed not to fight an external enemy, but to terrorize their own population.

The goal?

To create fear, chaos, and instability. Then to blame the violence on leftist political groups, especially communists and socialists. This psychological manipulation came to be known as the "**strategy of**

tension." The more terrified the public became, the more willing they were to accept authoritarian control in exchange for promises of safety.

"You had to attack civilians, the people, women, children, innocent people, unknown people far removed from any political game," explained Vincenzo Vinciguerra, former far-right terrorist and Gladio-linked informant. "The reason was quite simple: to force the public to turn to the state to ask for greater security."

Gladio operated in the shadows for decades, with intelligence services either turning a blind eye or actively supporting the operation. It wasn't until 1990, when Italian Prime Minister Giulio Andreotti officially acknowledged its existence, that the public learned the full scope of what had been done in their name.

What was shocking was not just what Gladio had done, but how familiar its methods would later feel.

Because the core of Gladio's approach—manufacturing chaos, cloaking the source, exploiting the aftermath—is exactly what we see now in **764**.

But this time, the battleground is not post-war Italy.

It's your child's browser.

Rituals Without Rationale

Where Gladio used bombs, **764** uses trauma. Where Gladio forged documents, **764** forges personas. Where Gladio blamed **The Com**munists, **764** doesn't bother with blame at all. It simply destroys.

And the result is eerily similar: a fractured, frightened public unsure of who the real enemy is, and increasingly willing to accept anyone who promises to restore order.

764 does not need to explain its purpose because it doesn't speak in manifestos. It speaks in mutilated children, livestreamed suicides, encrypted folders of spiritual pornography, and sadism as initiation.

If Gladio was state-backed terror masquerading as security, then **764** is spirit-backed collapse masquerading as chaos.

It is the same **strategy of tension**, but this time, the agents of destabilization aren't shadowy NATO operatives.

They're teenagers.

Worse, they're your teenagers.

Cultivating Crisis, Begging for Order

Whether or not **764** was born from any government or intelligence

In the late 1940s, secret paramilitary networks spread across Western Europe to act as underground resistance fighters in the event of a Soviet invasion. Italy's version of this network was called Operation Gladio.

program is irrelevant.

It follows the same logic.

Create unbearable social pressure. Induce terror. Destroy meaning. Corrupt the innocent. Then let the wound fester until the world cries out for a savior.

Gladio manufactured leftist terror to provoke a conservative response. **764** manufactures cultural collapse to provoke a spiritual submission.

These ritualists of ruin are not just wrecking the world for fun. They are grooming it for something to come.

Something that doesn't require explanation. Something that doesn't need to wear red robes or command an army.

Something that will walk through the door of chaos and offer to clean up the mess—for a price.

CHAPTER 9
HIDDEN IN THE ALGORITHM

I t's easy to imagine these cults operating in the shadows—in basements lit by flickering candles, in abandoned buildings, in the far reaches of the dark web. But the truth is far more terrifying: They're hiding in the light.

764 and its many offshoots don't need secrecy. They need saturation. And they've found it in the very platforms that claim to connect the world.

Platforms of Corruption

TikTok. Discord. Telegram. Reddit. Roblox. Steam. Twitter.

These are not just playgrounds or chat apps. They are recruitment tools, initiation chambers, and ritual theaters.

The same platform where your child posts dance videos or builds digital castles is the same one used to lure minors into group chats, where "challenges" begin and degradation escalates.

TikTok:

Short-form videos glamorize self-harm, eroticize submission, and mask ritualistic behavior in meme formats.

The online platforms that claim to connect the world are targeting our children with algorithms that glorify pain and death

Discord:

Private servers with coded names, such as "NightSchool" or "Temple Zero," host roleplay that can turn into real-life grooming.

Roblox and Minecraft:

Their private messaging features and custom game builds have been used to share ritual imagery, conduct initiation "quests," and mask adult-child contact.

Telegram and Matrix:

Encrypted chat apps serve as deep forums for **764** members, where images, videos, and "**cull lists**" are traded like currency.
The brilliance of **764** isn't that it invented a new internet.
It's that it's exploiting the one we already gave to our children.

Leaderless, Yet Everywhere

These aren't structured cults with robes, compound bunkers, or charismatic leaders.

They are networked mythologies, drawing power from the very absence of a chain of command.

764 spreads like a virus, not a sermon. Its members don't memorize doctrine—they perform it. They don't follow orders—they compete to be more extreme, more brutal, more "insightful."

It's a digital age cult—fluid, fast, and designed to survive detection.

No central server.

No formal leadership.

No clear boundaries between "jokes," "games," and genuine spiritual depravity.

It is gamified evil—and the prize is your child's soul.

The Paralysis of Institutions

Governments can barely keep up with cybercrime, let alone cyber-occultism. Few law enforcement agencies have units trained in symbolic extremism, esoteric ideology, or the digital psychological warfare deployed by these groups.

Tech platforms hide behind vague "terms of service" and mass-reporting loopholes. Even when reported, many of these groups are too decentralized to be banned effectively. Ban one channel and five more appear.

Mainstream media—so quick to decry misinformation—remains largely silent on this threat, often out of fear of being accused of stoking "moral panic." But this isn't panic. It's already reality.

Worse, every delay is a gift to the predators.

Now With Artificial Intelligence

The next phase is already here.

AI-generated deepfake content: Used to blackmail victims or stage fake rituals

Bots posing as teenagers: To draw in vulnerable users and channel them toward darker servers

Auto-generated **O9A** texts and sigils: Used to cloak propaganda in layers of gibberish

Algorithms don't care what they promote. They care about what gets engagement. And what gets engagement is often violent, shocking, or obscene.

764 thrives in this environment.

The system isn't just blind.

It's helping them hide.

The Final Camouflage

All of this—the memes, the emojis, the encrypted chats, the cosplay, the usernames that blend numbers and ancient symbols—isn't random.

It's ritual obfuscation.

The same way **O9A** invented arcane terms to bore outsiders and disorient critics, **764** uses irony, gamer slang, and internet culture as a veil of normalcy.

But by the time you realize what you're looking at, it's already too late.

Because they weren't trying to persuade you.

They were trying to reach your children.

And they already have.

CHAPTER 10

DIGITAL RITUALS EXPOSED

When Ryan Mauro, a renowned national security specialist, sat across from seasoned law enforcement agents and investigators, he noticed something unusual: fear. Not the kind you see in crime shows or behind bulletproof glass. This was quieter, heavier. The type of fear that comes from knowing you're up against something too big, too fast, and too monstrous to control.

That something is **764**.

Law enforcement doesn't just lack manpower—they lack the tools. Agencies admit their cyber squads are outmatched. **764**'s use of layered **VPNs**, **steganography**, Tor routing, and rapid rehosting means even when authorities shut down a server, a new one pops up before the ink dries on the report. In many cases, entire task forces rely on a single forensics analyst to comb through dozens of seized hard drives, some filled with encrypted horrors they may never be able to open.

And all the while, **764** continues to grow.

Since 2022, the network has siphoned $2.3 million from U.S. teens through romance scams, extortion, and **cryptocurrency** laundering. But money isn't the end game. It's just fuel for the real prize: suffering.

By 2025, **764** had amassed over 110,000 paying members, with

Prasan Neapl

core servers containing more than 500 terabytes of child sexual abuse content—an industrial-level atrocity never before seen in the digital age.

The Ritual Machine

764 doesn't operate like a traditional crime ring. It's a sadistic economy. A points-for-pain system where every act of humiliation or brutality becomes currency.

Members store edited clips of sexual abuse, self-harm, and animal torture into graphic files called "**Lorebooks**." These aren't just archives—they're status symbols. The more grotesque the content, the more valuable it becomes inside the cult.

When a **Lorebook** goes viral within **764**, its creator gains rank and is granted access to private channels such as **764 Inferno**, the elite inner circle.

Admins post informal scoreboards every week:

"Brad"— two suicides, five pet kills

"Trippy"—One suicide attempt, three cut-sign videos

These aren't statistics. They're digital trophies. And they drive competition.

High scorers get colored roles, direct chats with leadership, authority to issue group-wide "quests," and first pick of newly groomed victims. Stop contributing … and your privileges vanish.

This system doesn't just encourage violence. It demands it.

And the highest reward? A live-streamed suicide. Known as the "**endgame**," it offers instant elevation into the top tier of the cult. Some are even memorialized in pinned chats—icons of digital martyrdom.

Non-governmental organizations (NGOs) and federal agents now label **764** as something beyond sextortion or trafficking. It's ritual abuse wrapped in swastikas and pentagrams. A modern-day cult that feeds off despair.

The Rebirth Under Trippy

When founder Bradley Chance Cadenhead was imprisoned in 2023, it should have been a death blow. Instead, eighteen-year-old Prasan Nepal—known by his handle "Trippy"—rebooted the machine.

What followed was version 2.0 of **764.** Bigger. Brutal. Nearly bulletproof.

Nepal created a "core-and-spokes" model—an elite, invite-only hub on **Signal** and **Session**, with outer channels on **Discord**, **Telegram**, **TikTok**, and other platforms for grooming and crypto flows.

The Playbook & Quotas

He and co-leader Leonidas Varagiannis ("War") published a guidebook detailing weekly production targets. Every recruit was expected to submit a quota of content, including cut signs, animal mutilation, **CSAM**, and more.

Lorebooks as Currency

Now merged with gore and animal abuse, **Lorebooks** became a tradable commodity. The Department of Justice (DOJ) confirmed that these files were used as internal money, unlocking new ranks and privileges.

Nepal recorded tutorials on how to locate depressed teens via **Roblox**, **TikTok**, and **Discord**. Lower-level members handled grooming. He managed the vetting and wallets.

A Full Cash Engine

Victims were forced into "**pig butchering**" scams—romantic frauds designed to launder crypto into **Monero** wallets controlled by Nepal. This money paid for was used to purchase burner phones, new domains, and conduct **DDoS** (Distributed Denial of Service) attacks against watchdogs.

Integrated Terrorism

Nepal's handbook expanded the toolkit—**swatting**, bomb threats, live-streamed pet torture—all to shock victims and create new

Lorebook content. The FBI now classifies the network as "nihilistic violent extremism."

Plug-In to 'The Com'

Nepal tied **764** into the broader digital crime underworld, trading stolen identities and deepfakes for reach and revenue. This alliance gave **764** industrial-level resilience.

Why it Works

Psychological Leverage:

Victims battling depression are told their deaths will make someone a legend.

Ideological Confusion:

764 masks its ideology in **edgelord** slang and nihilism, appealing to the angry and alienated.

Platform Failure:

Apps like **Discord** make it easy to create new accounts and servers, rendering bans ineffective.

Safety Warnings for Families

Watch for secrecy and mood swings among family members— recruitment can take just days.

Look for cut signs, especially "**764**" or recruiter usernames.

Report threatening messages immediately (988 Lifeline, NCMEC, FBI field office).

Use device-level controls to prevent hidden app installs.

Phrases like "cut for the scoreboard," "+1 suicide," or "**Lorebook** drop" must be treated as red alerts.

A Cult with No Leader

In April 2025, Nepal and Varagiannis were arrested by the U.S. Department of Justice. Their arrest revealed just how centralized the **764 Inferno** core had become.

But since then, the group has splintered. No new leader has emerged. Instead, rotating admins manage smaller cells across encrypted platforms.

And with every week that passes, another teen is targeted.

The Fear Is Justified

Ryan Mauro was right. Law enforcement is afraid. Not because they're weak, but because they're human. They are trying to fight digital demons with analog weapons—and falling behind.

The answer? Exposure. Pressure. Action. A federal task force dedicated to this threat. A documentary that forces the public to look. A movement of churches and families that refuses to stay silent.

Because **764** isn't slowing down.

And neither can we.

CHAPTER 11

THE COM: A NETWORK OF DIGITAL PREDATORS

If **764** is the cult, then **The Com** is the cathedral.

It is the unholy convergence point where child predators, digital con artists, gore-peddlers, political extremists, and occult **accelerationist**s come together—not to worship a god, but to serve disorder itself.

Unlike **764**, **The Com** doesn't care about aesthetics. There are no digital emblems, symbols, or badges. No cut-sign rituals. No leaderboard of suicides. What **The Com** offers is something far more powerful:

Infrastructure.

Servers. Scripts. Laundering tools. Recruits. Victims. Leverage.

The Com is a decentralized, encrypted marketplace, a loose confederation of malicious actors trading content, data, access, and pain. Some are motivated by profit, others by ideology, still others by nothing more than sadistic pleasure. What binds them is functionality:

If you have something to trade—be it **CSAM**, gore, hacked credit card dumps, **swatting** services, or a newly-groomed teenager—**The Com** will welcome you.

A Web Without a Spider

There is no leader. No manifesto. No dark overlord behind the curtain. Rather than an organization, **The Com** is an emergent network, the digital version of a criminal bazaar.

Participants create private **Telegram** groups, burner **Discord** channels, and invite-only **Signal** hubs. When one gets taken down, another is born. Like mold, it thrives in darkness and feeds off decay.

Its culture is pure decentralization. Each cell operates independently, but taps into a shared economy of stolen identities, **cryptocurrency** tools, and abuse content.

This is where **764** found its second life.

After Prasan Nepal's arrest, the **764** surviving members didn't scatter in fear—they migrated deeper into **The Com**, forging alliances and acquiring resources. From there, **764** splinter cells launched their own operations, recruiting, grooming, laundering, and broadcasting anew.

What Gets Traded in The Com

Child sex abuse material (CSAM) and Gore Vaults:

Gigabytes of child abuse material, **blood porn**, and animal torture clips—sold or traded for clout.

Stolen IDs:

Victim credentials, especially those of children, are used to open **cryptocurrency** accounts or create fake profiles.

Swatting & Threat Services:

Want to harass a parent or rival? **The Com** is ready to provide bomb-threat robocalls, school lockdown tools, and police raid hoaxes on demand.

Deepfakes and AI Porn:

Face-swapping tools to create synthetic child pornography—untraceable, yet no less damaging.

Crypto-Laundering Tunnels:

Monero mixers, fake charities, and foreign wallet farms to move money invisibly.

Recruitment Scripts:

Prewritten dialogues and grooming guides to be used on **Discord**,

Roblox, **TikTok**, or **Minecraft**.

Why It Survives

Resilience Through Redundancy: The Com doesn't die when one channel is nuked. It regenerates. Automatically.

Talent Sharing: One cell's bomb-maker becomes another's sextortion coach. Groomers trade tactics. Coders share exploits.

Ideological Ambiguity: While **764** has a dark spiritual goal, most Com members don't care. This ambiguity makes alliances easy.

Market Incentives: Success is rewarded—money, influence, anonymity. And in this world, that's all the incentive most need.

The Bigger Picture

The existence of **The Com** forces a reckoning: this is no longer about a single cult, or even a few bad actors. This is an ecosystem of radicalized sadism.

And the tools it uses—AI, crypto, social platforms, anonymity services—aren't going away.

That means our response must evolve.

Law enforcement needs:

- Multi-agency digital predator task forces
- Faster forensics on encrypted drives
- Legislative teeth to prosecute steganographic file traders
- Cybercrime squads trained not just in tech, but in cultic behavior

This is not just about catching criminals. It's about dismantling an infrastructure built for digital evil.

Conclusion

The Com is not a myth. It's not a conspiracy. It's the very real backbone of the internet's most dangerous predators.

764 may have shocked the world. But **The Com** explains why **764** exists—and why its horror keeps returning.

Until we confront this predator marketplace for what it is—a cartel of chaos—we'll remain on defense.

And our children will remain the hunted.

CHAPTER 12

COOL VIOLENCE:
WHEN THE RANDOM ISN'T RANDOM

O n June 10, 2025, in the quiet city of Sunrise, Florida, a family gathering turned into a nightmare. Fiorella Lopez's seventy-five-year-old mother was walking to a birthday celebration—unaware that a man was watching her.

Shirtless and pacing, he stood just two doors down from their home. Lopez's sister, waiting at the entrance, sensed something was off and tried to **Signal** her mother to be cautious.

Hurtado Florez

It was too late.

The man—later identified as Carlos Hurtado Florez, age 26—grabbed the elderly woman by the collar and slammed a frying pan into her skull. She fell to the pavement. Her son ran to help, only to be attacked himself.

Florez smashed the man's head, leaving him bloodied and broken beside his mother.

Florez had already attacked his own brother and vandalized a car just moments before the sidewalk ambush. His crime spree had no apparent motive. No theft. No demands. No words exchanged—just random, blunt-force violence in the middle of the day.

Police later charged Florez with aggravated battery on a person sixty-five years or older, aggravated assault with a deadly weapon, false imprisonment, and multiple counts of battery.

The Lopez family, which had fled Venezuela seeking safety and peace in America, now lived in fear.

"I came here for peace," said Fiorella. "We never imagined something like this could happen to our mother."

And then there was the tattoo—"CooL"—etched beneath Florez's right eye.

To most, it would seem meaningless. Maybe even goofy. However, to those who study the **764** network, that tattoo should set off alarm bells.

Reading Between the Lines (and the Letters)

Stylized tattoos using zeroes instead of letters are common in digital subcultures—especially among extremists looking to conceal messages in plain sight. "CooL" may look harmless, but "Coo" is potentially shorthand for **The Com**—the shadowy leadership council that guides **764**'s ideology, logistics, and chaos campaigns.

It's doubtful the average police officer would recognize the reference. In fact, many small departments across America likely have no awareness of **The Com** at all, let alone its cryptic calling cards. Obfuscation is part of the strategy. Make your symbols look innocuous. Brand your chaos with irony. Hide your loyalty in pop-culture camouflage.

Whether or not Florez is a formal member of **The Com** doesn't even matter. His attack—utterly random, incredibly violent, and deeply traumatic—accomplishes the very goals **The Com** desires: tear down public trust, destroy peace of mind, and spread trauma like wildfire.

Don't Dismiss It as Madness

The public and the press are quick to write off such violence as the work of the mentally ill. That's understandable. After all, you'd have to be unwell to beat a grandmother with a frying pan for no reason.

But here's the more profound truth: you'd have to be unwell to join **The Com**, too.

And that's what makes it so dangerous. **The Com** is a magnet for the mentally unstable, the sociopathic, the broken. But instead of therapy or medication, it gives them **Atomwaffen** ideology, **Telegram** channels, and a sense of purpose rooted in destruction.

It's not just a support group for the unwell; it's a militant asylum that replaces healing with hatred, and remorse with ritualized cruelty. It creates meaning out of mayhem.

So, when Americans ask, "Why are these attacks happening?"— the answer isn't just mental illness. It's that someone is offering these unstable minds a reason to act on their worst impulses.

Whether Carlos Florez knew what his tattoo really meant, or if it was just another sign of his unraveling mind, the effect was the same:

Another family is shattered. Another community is traumatized. Another brick is chipped away from the foundation of civil society.

That's **The Com**'s mission. And this was its message.

Some crimes feel senseless. Pointless. Random.

But when you start to see patterns—in targets, in tactics, in timing—it becomes clear: The violence isn't random at all. It's curated chaos.

This is the signature of **The Com**.

A network that thrives on stochastic, or seemingly random, violence that cloaks itself in irony, memes, and misdirection. That trains its members to harm, not to gain territory or riches—but to confuse, demoralize, and collapse society.

The Syringe Stabbings in France

Take the shocking case from June 2025.

During the annual Fêtes de la Musique—a massive, open-air celebration across France—145 concertgoers were stabbed with syringes, many of them teenage girls. The attacks were reported across multiple cities, with several victims hospitalized. Authorities arrested twelve suspects, but what disturbed investigators most was the sheer coordination of the event:

Multiple cities. One night.

All targeting a chaotic, overstimulated public gathering.

Weapons that induced panic, symbolized control, and evoked fears of drugging or infection.

No ransom. No manifesto. Just widespread fear. A terrorist act without the usual ideological branding.

Except there may have been one—hidden in encrypted forums.

Insiders have noted that this exact kind of operation—decentralized, horrific, and laced with viral panic—fits **The Com**'s swarm-style playbook. If members of a cell like **764, No Lives Matter**, or **NMK** (Not My Kids) were behind this, the motivations may not have been political at all.

It may have been a "quest."

One that earned its perpetrators **"Points for Pain."**

Videos of panicked victims. Screen grabs of emergency alerts. A clip of someone crying in confusion. These are not just byproducts. They may be the trophies—traded in **Lorebook** vaults or used to level up inside private channels like **764 Inferno**.

And the syringe? That wasn't just a weapon. It was a statement: A symbol of violation, chaos, and state impotence. A weapon that terrifies without leaving an obvious motive trail.

Investigators in France and across Europe are still combing through digital breadcrumbs. But one thing is clear: if **The Com** was involved, this wasn't about the victims.

It was about the message—and the fear that followed.

Because to them, it's not senseless violence. It's performance art with a purpose:

Collapse society. Confuse the systems. And keep it all looking like madness—until it's too late to put the pieces back together.

CHAPTER 13

AGENTS OF CHAOS:
THE DEVIL'S DIGITAL SOLDIERS

In the war between Heaven and Hell, Satan does not wait for consensus or coordination. He thrives in chaos, revels in confusion, and wields disorder as both weapon and disguise.

And in the digital age, the battlefield has expanded.

Today's enemies are not always marching in columns with flags, nor meeting in secret societies with ritual oaths. They're livestreaming. Coding. Messaging. **Doxxing. Swatting**. Killing.

They are the foot soldiers of disorder—knowingly or unknowingly working toward the same unholy goal: the collapse of civilization to make way for the **Antichrist**.

Let's be clear. Satan's army is not composed solely of men in black robes gathered around goat-head idols. Sometimes, it looks like a lonely teenager behind a keyboard.

Or a man with a knife in a shopping aisle. Or a pickup truck on a crowded street.

Satan does not care whether his chaos is executed by an organized terrorist cell or a "lone wolf" madman.

So long as society buckles, truth is buried, and fear reigns, the plan advances.

A Bloody Trail of Co-Conspirators

Take, for example, Bradford James Gille, a name that may be forgotten in the next news cycle, but whose actions echo with spiritual consequence.

In July 2025, Gille stormed into a Walmart in Traverse City, Michigan, stabbing eleven innocent people seemingly at random. No manifesto. No known ideology. Just madness, mayhem, and blood in the aisles of a place meant for diapers and discount groceries.

Then there was Shamsud-Din Jabbar, who flew an ISIS flag from the back of his pickup truck and barreled down Bourbon Street in New Orleans on New Year's Day 2025.

He killed fourteen and wounded fifty-seven. Crowds that gathered to ring in a new year were instead ushered into horror, grief, and trauma—each scream, each bloodstain another brick in the Devil's dark cathedral.

Or consider the online group known as **Purgatory**—not the theological concept, but a digital cell of young men that weaponized police departments by filing false emergency reports across the nation.

From schools to casinos, airports to homes, they triggered **swatting** with armed raids, mass evacuations, and panic. Their members—Evan Strauss, Owen Jarboe, and Brayden Grace—weren't preaching revolution. They weren't even offering reasons. But the effects were indistinguishable from terrorism: the psychological breakdown of trust, the saturation of fear, and the normalization of lawless, random danger.

A Common Thread: Destruction by Design

These men may never have met. They may never have read the same forums, belonged to the same cults, or heard the same voices in their heads. But they are co-conspirators nonetheless, connected not by collaboration, but by consequence.

They are the hands that strike, the voices that scream, the keystrokes that dismantle. And the puppet master behind them?

Satan himself.

Whether it's the occult-driven goals of the **Order of Nine Angles**, the anonymity-wrapped evil of **764**, or the shadowy digital warfare orchestrated by networks like **The Com**, the goal remains unchanged: create enough pain, confusion, terror, and chaos until the world begs for a "savior."

And then Satan will offer one.

Not Christ. Not truth. But a counterfeit:

The **Antichrist**.

A global figure who promises peace but delivers bondage. Who claims to restore order, but only under the condition of total allegiance. And the world—exhausted, terrified, and spiritually starved—will welcome him with open arms.

Unless ...

The Restraining Force

The Apostle Paul gives us a vital insight in 2 Thessalonians 2:6-7: *"And now you know what is holding him back, so that he may be revealed at the proper time. For the secret power of lawlessness is already at work; but the one who now holds it back will continue to do so till he is taken out of the way."*

Let that sink in:

"The secret power of lawlessness is already at work."

That's exactly what we are witnessing today.

It's not always obvious. It doesn't always wear horns or wave flags. It's often secret, hidden, anonymous, encrypted, or disguised as madness. But it is lawlessness—a spiritual assault on the moral order of creation, and it's already moving through the culture like poison in the bloodstream.

Whether it's Bradford James Gille's bloody knife in a aisle in the local Walmart ...

Or Shamsud-Din Jabbar's ISIS truck plowing through New Year's celebrants ...

Or the **Purgatory** gang hijacking 911 systems to flood police departments with lies...

... The goal is always the same: **Destroy law and order**—because without it, Satan has a clear runway to introduce his false messiah.

Satan doesn't need these groups to coordinate. He needs them to **corrode**. Their lawlessness isn't just a symptom of evil—it is the system he's building.

The machine is running. The only thing stopping it is the Church.

This "restrainer," though debated among theologians, is widely believed to be the Holy Spirit, the Church, or the hand of God-ordained governance. Regardless of the interpretation, the message is clear: Evil has limits, and those limits are enforced by those who resist.

The "restrainer" could most likely be the Church—and as it weakens, lawlessness grows. And so does the power of Satan.

Which means this: The Church isn't here to spectate. **We are the firewall**. We are the last line of defense before the floodgates of Hell break wide open.

Scripture urges us to remain vigilant. As Peter warned:
"Be alert and of sober mind. Your enemy the Devil prowls around like a roaring lion looking for someone to devour."

(1 Peter 5:8-9)

And James reminds us of our authority:
"Submit yourselves, then, to God. Resist the Devil, and he will flee from you."

(James 4:7)

The Church's Mission: Impede the Gates of Hell

This is not simply about preaching on Sundays or avoiding sin in private life. This is about spiritual and legal warfare.

It means exposing networks like **764**.

It means holding governments accountable when they fund or enable chaos.

It means building digital tools of our own—righteous ones—to combat the devil's tech warfare.

It means creating laws and reforms that prevent madmen from livestreaming slaughter or organizing terror in encrypted chatrooms.

And it means praying, standing, and refusing to back down—even when the world tells us resistance is futile.

Satan's agents are clever. Some wear suits. Some wear hoodies. Some wear no expression at all. But their work is unmistakable. It is the drumbeat of the end times. And the only thing that will hold it back … is us.

The Church.

Resisting. Exposing. Fighting.

Not for survival—but for truth.

Not just to delay the **Antichrist**, but to glorify Christ—until the day He returns, not in anonymity, but in power.

CHAPTER 14
WHISPERS IN THE HALLS

They should know. They should all know.

Technology companies. School counselors. Federal agencies. Law enforcement Even the nonprofits that claim to protect children. They should all know.

But what's worse: Even those who do know, don't speak out. At least not publicly. Not forcefully. And certainly not as if the house was on fire. Welcome to the silence that sustains **764**.

Even after arrests. Even after congressional briefings. Even after major media outlets like ABC News and Reuters

Researcher Ryan Mauro: He found paralysis instead of ignorance

began reporting on the cult's international footprint, the institutions charged with protecting children remain, at best, subdued.

Ryan Mauro has spoken with agents, analysts, and tech executives behind closed doors. What he found wasn't ignorance—it was paralysis. Some are terrified of naming the group publicly, worried that doing so will **Signal** to **764** that they're under surveillance. Others admit they're simply outgunned.

Quite frankly, we're treating arson with a garden hose.

In interviews with tech professionals tasked with scanning for abusive material, the same story repeats: they see the content. They know what **Lorebooks** are. They are familiar with the **764** sigil. But they've been told not to speak of it. Not by law, but by a chilling kind of corporate risk aversion—one where public acknowledgment of this kind of evil could be seen as liability.

Some nonprofits are no better. They're willing to condemn trafficking. They'll issue statements about sextortion. But the moment ritual abuse, esoteric ideology, or references to the **Order of Nine Angles** enter the conversation, they clam up. It's too fringe. And they don't want to scare donors.

The silence is strategic. And it benefits only one side.

764 has learned to exploit this information vacuum. When victims try to report what's happening, they're often met with confused or dismissive responses. Who would believe a teenager claiming they were forced into cutting symbols and participating in a suicide leaderboard?

Worse still, educators and law enforcement aren't being briefed. In schools, guidance counselors know how to spot signs of bullying— but not ritual grooming. Most parents are unfamiliar with the term "**Lorebook**."

This is how cults flourish: not just in shadows, but in the silence.

The fear Mauro saw in those halls wasn't just about the crimes. It was about complicity—knowing what's out there and choosing not to sound the alarm.

If nothing changes, these whispers will one day become screams.

Because if we don't shout the truth, **764** will keep writing its gospel in the blood of our children—with the aim of crashing society and ushering the onset of the **Galactic Imperium**.

CHAPTER 15
THE GALACTIC IMPERIUM

It sounds like science fiction, a phrase stolen from pulp novels or the delusions of some D-list cult leader. But for the **Order of Nine Angles** and the networks it helped spawn, the **Galactic Imperium** is no joke. It is their promised future. Their final destination.

And it is drenched in blood.

According to **O9A** doctrine, the current era—our modern world—is diseased. The solution, they teach, is not reform but annihilation. Societal collapse is not an unfortunate consequence of their actions. It is the goal. Why? Because only from the ashes of this "corrupt civilization" can the **Galactic Imperium** rise.

This Imperium is not metaphorical. **O9A** texts describe it as a literal space-faring empire led by a spiritually evolved elite. These elites are not born but forged—through murder, rape, deceit, and ritual.

They call this process the **Seven-Fold Way**, a gauntlet of increasingly horrific "tests" meant to harden the soul into something ... post-human.

The **Galactic Imperium** is, at its core, a vision of eugenics by fire. An empire of psychopathic elites ruling over a burned-out world where empathy is weakness and cruelty is strength. It is the antithesis of the Kingdom of God. Where Revelation promises a new Heaven and a new Earth built upon justice and divine glory, the **Galactic**

63

Imperium promises iron rule through terror.

In this twisted theology, every act of violence is a stepping stone. Every ritual, every rape, every manipulated suicide, is seen as forward motion. Toward what? The forging of the Übermensch. The birth of the **Sithian** ruler. The crowning of the **Antichrist**.

There are no economic plans. No treaties. No utopian blueprints. Only destruction. **O9A**, **764**, and **The Com** don't bother to offer a vision of how the world should be. Because in their eyes, what matters is who reigns after the flames.

And it will not be the meek.

The idea of a **Galactic Imperium**, while absurd to sane ears, serves a crucial function: it gives cult members a purpose. It spiritualizes their violence. It creates a myth to live by, and a hell to march toward.

When **O9A** texts speak of **Aeonic Evolution**, this is their **endgame**. A world reordered not by persuasion, but by predation; not by progress, but by pain. It is what David Myatt, writing under the name Anton Long, envisioned not merely as a political revolution, but as a cosmic realignment.

Sound familiar?

It should. Because Revelation warns us: *"And they worshipped the beast, saying, Who is like unto the beast? Who is able to make war with him?"* (Revelation 13:4)

In **O9A**'s **Galactic Imperium**, the beast is not just welcomed. He is crowned.

The question is not whether this Imperium will succeed. The question is how many souls it will claim before it collapses under its own depravity.

Because if we do not resist this gospel of brutality, we may find that the Imperium has already begun—not in the stars, but in our schools, our chatrooms, our living rooms.

And by the time we look up, the beast may already be seated on his throne.

CHAPTER 16

THE CHOSEN EXECUTIONERS

The Chosen Executioners of **764 Inferno** are more than just online sadists; they are the twisted priesthood of a new demonic religion. With their "points-for-pain" system and grotesque rituals—like the $700 **Monero**-funded self-harm livestream we exposed in Chapter 11—they glorify agony and mock the sacred. These aren't mere acts of cruelty. They are sacraments of spiritual rebellion.

Their goal? To desecrate, to corrupt, and to hollow out the souls of the young. Just as 2 Thessalonians 2:9-10 warns of "wickedness that deceives those who are perishing." They seduce vulnerable minds into self-mutilation, hollowing them out for the spiritual collapse that paves the way for the **Antichrist**. This is the world they crave—one ruled by their so-called "**Galactic Imperium**" (see Chapter 13), where pain is holy and evil wears a crown.

But the Church is not called to retreat. We are called to resist. James 4:7 says it plainly: *"Submit yourselves therefore to God. Resist the devil, and he will flee from you."* That resistance starts with truth. It starts with exposure. These digital priests of despair must be unmasked—for the sake of our children, and the soul of a generation.

As previously discussed, **The Com** is a network—a decentralized, sprawling, protean beast that functions as an umbrella for the most deranged, sadistic, and extremist factions on Earth. It is a **Hydra**:

The Com is the umbrella organization for the most
deranged, sadistic, and extremist factions

sever one head, and two more grow in its place. A takedown here or there does nothing to stop the collective.

It is not simply big. It is galactic in scale.

And if the **Galactic Imperium** is the throne, **The Com** may be its priesthood—a false savior, whether the **Antichrist** for Christians or a tyrannical figure for others.

They aren't hiding anymore.

The Com used to be just whispers in the darkest corners of the internet. A muttering on obscure forums. A flash of gore behind **VPN** walls. A rumor circulated among cops and analysts who couldn't bring themselves to say it aloud.

Not anymore.

Now, its members are standing up in mugshots. Getting sentenced in federal courts. Leaving digital footprints across multiple continents.

And yet, despite arrests, leaks, and mounting awareness, one thing remains mostly undisturbed:

The belief among many of **The Com**'s members that they are destined to rule.

The Com as a Proto-Elite

If the **Order of Nine Angles** gave **The Com** its spiritual scaffolding, and **764** gave it its bloody tactics, **The Com** has evolved into something even more dangerous: a self-ordained aristocracy for a coming empire.

They don't see themselves as criminals. They see themselves as initiates. Pioneers of a new morality. Priests of chaos. Soldiers in the first wave of a total societal collapse—a collapse they believe is necessary, even righteous.

And when the smoke clears, they plan to rise.

The **Galactic Imperium**, the end-stage fantasy of **O9A** ideology, is often described in esoteric terms. A future **Aeon** ruled not by governments or religions, but by the most "evolved" individuals— those who have passed through the crucible of transgression and emerged stronger —those who proved their willingness to kill, to dominate, to destroy the old world entirely.

Who better to fill that role than **The Com**?

They've already killed. They've already conquered digital landscapes. They've already made children into sacrifices and boasted about it.

Now, they believe they've earned their place.

A Throne Built on blood

It is not difficult to imagine how this ideology could be co-opted by something even darker. The Book of Revelation speaks of a time when a global figure will rise to power, perform signs, demand worship, and declare war on the saints. Christians will be hunted, persecuted, martyred, and betrayed. The machinery of death will not be faceless. It will have soldiers.

If the **Galactic Imperium** is the throne, **The Com** imagines itself as the palace guard.

Not just killers. Chosen executioners.

Pre-installed Depravity

What makes **The Com** even more dangerous is how it has pre-adapted itself to this role. Its members have already proven their loyalty to destruction. Through **Lorebooks**. Through **CSAM** networks. Through livestreamed abuse. Through blackmail. Through manipulation. Through torture.

Unlike traditional military regimes or revolutionary guards, **The Com** doesn't require training. It doesn't require indoctrination. It is already brutal. Already eager. Already thirsty for permission to do what it has only done in secret.

Imagine the moment the secret is sanctified. When a leader arises and says, "What you once did in the shadows, you now do in my name."

The Gospel of Collapse

Their crimes, once shameful even to whisper about, are now badges of honor in their circles. Members of **764** already treat sadism like a scoreboard. They exchange gore files as currency. They livestream harm for social capital. Their cruelty is performative, efficient, and structured.

They are not just psychologically damaged. They are religiously motivated in the worst sense of the term. They see pain as a path to power. The gospel of collapse says: Destroy everything holy. Desecrate the innocent. Only then will the **New Aeon** arrive.

Weaponized for Revelation

It should be chilling to any reader of Scripture that a group of self-appointed murderers has already volunteered to be the executioners of a new world order. The **Antichrist** wouldn't need to build a Gestapo. He wouldn't need to train a secret police. He already has them.

They're not waiting for a paycheck. They're waiting for a **Signal**.

A Warning and a Call

These acts echo the "false signs and wonders" of Matthew 24:24.

This is no longer just a digital cult. It is an army in waiting. A network of nodes, quietly growing, refining its brutality, and daring the world to ignore them—until it's too late.

Unless we confront this now—not just as a criminal enterprise, but as a spiritual threat—we may find ourselves in a world where the lawless are the lawmakers, and those who kill the most are given the crown.

The Chosen Executioners are here.

And they believe the kingdom is coming.

To resist this sadistic priesthood, see the Appendix for practical tools to protect children and expose digital evil.

CHAPTER 17

LOREBOOK NATIONS

There was a time when the internet was a place of innocence and curiosity. In this space, families shared recipes, schoolkids built GeoCities pages, and dial-up tones preceded the wonder of instant connection.

That internet is long dead.

What has replaced it is a digital wasteland increasingly shaped by cruelty as entertainment and anonymity as power. And at the heart of that cultural shift is something few have heard of, but many have seen: the **Lorebook**.

Originally coined within the **764** cult, **Lorebooks** began as encrypted archives of pain—zip files packed with self-harm footage, coerced child sexual abuse, suicide recordings, animal torture, and acts of ritual humiliation. They weren't just documentation; they were currency. **Points for Pain**. Trophies in a competition for digital dominance.

Points for Pain wasn't just a phrase—it was the engine that drove **764**'s culture. Each act of violence or humiliation captured on video wasn't random; it was a means of climbing the internal hierarchy. Members weren't just seeking shock value. They were earning status.

A coerced photo might earn a user access to a private chat room.

A self-harm clip might unlock the next level of community prestige. But the ultimate prize—what insiders referred to as "instant tier elevation"—came from coercing a suicide on camera. That single act was the golden chalice of notoriety in **764**.

The system functioned like a twisted video game. Contributors were ranked. Their usernames are listed alongside kill counts, **cut-sign** captures, and pet torture stats. **Lorebooks** containing this content were passed around like digital medals. And just like a competitive leaderboard, those at the top were envied, praised, and feared.

The psychological toll on victims was devastating. Survivors report being told they were worth "points," reduced to a score in someone else's game. Some were even forced to write messages like "+1 suicide" or carve **764** sigils into their bodies to validate the abuser's credibility within the network.

This point system isn't just sadism. It is a strategy. It trains young recruits to become hunters. It converts pain into social currency. And it ensures a constant stream of content to fuel the cult's reputation and growth.

But now, Lorebook culture is metastasizing. You don't have to be part of **764** to be infected by its influence.

On fringe forums, **Discord** servers, **Reddit** threads, and increasingly even on mainstream platforms like **TikTok** or **X**, the aesthetic of "edgy sadism" is spreading like a virus. Users post short, dehumanizing clips of violence layered with ironic memes. Suicide baiting is passed off as dark humor. Videos of self-harm get thousands of views and comments praising the cuts as "art."

The **Lorebook** has left the vault and entered the bloodstream.

A new generation is being raised in a digital jungle where the reward is cruelty, and the goal is collapse. And they're learning this not in secret rooms, but in public threads. In comment sections. In the "for you" feed. **764** may have pioneered the system, but countless unaffiliated teens and young adults now echo the behavior without even knowing the origin.

Some call it copycat culture. Others call it memetic warfare. But it's far more insidious.

Because what **764** did was not merely create a file-sharing ring. They built a theology of sadism. A worldview where domination, exploitation, and emotional collapse are signs of strength. Where

Known as "White Tiger," this man orchestrated one of the worst-known cases of cyber-grooming in German history

empathy is a weakness. Where "the game" is to cause maximum psychological damage—and be rewarded with status for it.

And that game is being taught to millions, one post at a time.

This is why digital safety efforts that focus solely on parental controls or nudity filters often fall short. They treat symptoms, not systems. The spread of **Lorebook** Nation isn't just a tech problem, it's a spiritual one. It's a revival of cruelty as a public virtue. A digital echo of the Roman Coliseum—except now the blood is visible in the present, and the audience never logs off.

What's most disturbing is how effective the model has become. Gamified pain. An algorithmic reward system for degradation. And all of it scalable, shareable, rehostable. You take one down, three more appear. Not because they're all part of **764**—but because they've adopted its ethos.

And in that way, the cult wins.

Because the **Lorebook** was never just a file. It was a philosophy. And now it's a nation without borders, silently recruiting your children through likes, shares, and upvotes.

One of the most horrifying illustrations of this was the arrest of "White Tiger," a 20-year-old German-Iranian man in Hamburg, Germany. Known online as a prolific member of the **764** network, White Tiger orchestrated one of the worst-known cases of cyber-grooming in German history.

His crimes spanned continents—abusing at least eight minors across Germany, the United States, Canada, and the UK. Using threats, manipulation, and blackmail, he coerced victims into recording extreme self-harm and sexual content, some involving carved "cut signs" into their skin.

His most notorious act was demanding a thirteen-year-old American boy livestream his suicide. These acts weren't just recorded—they were stored, scored, and shared within **764**'s **Lorebooks** as digital trophies.

When law enforcement finally moved in, it took over a year of cyber-forensic work, tips from the FBI, and encrypted communications to build a case strong enough to act. The damage, however, had already been done. The Lorebook had claimed more lives for the sake of points, prestige, and perversion.

To fight this, we cannot merely report and restrict. We must reveal. Preach. Warn. Expose. Because the only firewall stronger than shame is truth. And the only antidote to this gospel of destruction is the Gospel of life.

CHAPTER 18
THE SHADOW DOCTRINE

A t the center of **764**'s strategy lies an unwritten rulebook—one they never name, never share, and never admit exists. But its fingerprints are everywhere. This is the **Shadow Doctrine**.

It is not a manifesto. It is not posted in a forum or stored in a PDF file. It is a culture of silence and survival, passed through implication and imitation, guiding members toward maximum damage while preserving plausible deniability. It is how a decentralized hive of sadists, extortionists, and occultists functions like a disciplined army.

The first rule of the **Shadow Doctrine** is: You do not talk about the **Shadow Doctrine**.

This isn't just a cliché—it's a tactic. Silence is not just protection; it is a form of power. By refusing to centralize their beliefs, **764** becomes a moving target. There is no head to cut off, no text to quote, no doctrine to ban. Every act of violence, every **Lorebook**, every new victim, becomes the doctrine. They preach through carnage.

The second rule: Obscurity is armor.

Members are trained to camouflage their intent. They speak in riddles. They embed messages in memes. They write nothing in plain English that could be used in court. Their language is a cipher meant to exhaust and mislead investigators. The more confusing they appear, the less likely anyone will make the effort to decode them. (Which is precisely why a glossary is included in this book.)

This is why references to "**Lorebooks**," "**cut-signs**," or even group names like "**764 Inferno**" seem to mutate constantly. Like a digital Proteus, the network shifts shapes just as authorities begin to get a grip. It is by design.

This tactic has roots. **O9A**, which helped inspire **764**, was notorious for flooding its literature with faux-academic jargon, invented mythologies, and meaningless neologisms—new expressions or meanings for words.

The goal wasn't clarity. It was confusion. Overwhelm the reader. Bury the horrors in 10,000 words of esoteric nonsense.

764 took that playbook and turned it into a smokescreen.

A third rule: Doctrine is downstream of damage.

While most ideologies explain their vision first and act second, **764** reverses the order. They act violently and let the explanation follow later, if at all. Their members don't ask why. They ask how much. How far. How many. It is action before thought, pain before philosophy.

This, too, serves a purpose. Without a central creed, members avoid infighting. They don't argue over strategy or end goals. The goal is the act itself: destruction, chaos, collapse.

There is no debate because there is no destination—just acceleration. Which leads to the fourth and final rule: Shadow is sacred.

To these groups, visibility is vulnerability. They view light not as truth but as exposure. Anyone who tries to shine light on them is mocked, hacked, or swatted. Journalists, watchdogs, and whistleblowers are targets not just because they threaten security, but because they violate the sanctity of the dark.

In the lore of groups like **O9A**, secrecy itself is holy. To hide is to prove one's worth. To remain hidden while causing harm is to become transcendent. **764** has adopted this principle as a core tenet. It is not enough to destroy. One must do so without ever being seen.

This is why the cult spreads like ink in water. It has no fixed shape. No public leaders. No printed scripture. Just a network of masked disciples following a doctrine no one can prove exists—because it lives only in the shadow.

And that, ultimately, is what makes **764** and its affiliates the most dangerous cult of the digital age.

Because their religion is not built on belief. It is built on silence, sadism, and the sanctity of never being caught.

CHAPTER 19
THE PRICE OF EVIL

R unning a global terror network that targets children isn't just immoral—it's expensive.

Encrypted servers, burner phones, secure apps, bulletproof hosting, and rapid re-homing after takedowns all require one thing: money money, and lots of it. The disturbing truth is that evil has a price tag, and **764** has found a way to pay it.

While many still imagine the group as a ragtag band of loners sharing grotesque memes in the shadows, the reality is far more sophisticated. The modern **764** cell is a self-sustaining ecosystem. It grooms, it extorts, it terrorizes—and it monetizes.

A Digital Hydra with an Operating Budget

Every time a server gets shut down, another rises in its place. That agility isn't magic—it's money ringleaders pay for offshore domains, rotate through layers of **VPNs**, and utilize end-to-end encrypted platforms that offer premium-level anonymity for a fee. They invest in Distributed Denial of Service (**DDoS**) protection and dark-net rehosting services to ensure longevity; some even lease server time from infrastructure hubs in hostile nations.

This is not operated on spare change.

So where does the money all come from?

The funding begins with the victims themselves. Many are not only exploited sexually and psychologically, but also financially. Children coerced into creating abuse content are later manipulated into "**tribute payments**"—sending **cryptocurrency** to their abuser as proof of loyalty, submission, or silence. In some cases, these payments aren't voluntary at all. They're extorted through blackmail, threats, and psychological warfare.

Others are turned into mules. Members of **764** coach victims—especially teenagers—in how to launder money, move funds through crypto wallets, or even open accounts for fraud and romance scams. They are transformed from prey into tools.

Enter **Monero**.

Monero is a **cryptocurrency** similar to **Bitcoin**—but with a significant difference: total anonymity.

Unlike **Bitcoin**, which records every transaction on a public ledger (albeit without revealing names), **Monero** employs advanced cryptographic techniques to conceal transaction origins, destinations, and amounts. This makes it nearly impossible to trace. It's the currency of choice for criminals who want to vanish into the digital ether.

With **Monero**, **764** can receive payments, buy new domains, rent bulletproof hosting, purchase phishing kits, and even acquire stolen identities—all without leaving a financial trail. The network's handlers are familiar with transferring money across borders using mixers, decentralized exchanges, and dark web services. One arrest or seizure won't stop the flow. Their financial pipeline is decentralized, deniable, and durable.

But they don't just rely on tech.

Victims themselves are forced into what investigators call "**pig-butchering** scams"—a type of romance fraud where a scammer builds an emotional relationship with the target, then slowly drains their finances under the guise of a fake investment opportunity. Girls recruited online are ordered to play the role of scammers, their scripts written by **764** leaders, the funds funneled back to the group's crypto wallets.

And when that's not enough, they turn to data theft, stolen credit cards, and outright extortion. Screenshots of a victim's private messages or photos become ransom notes. If the victim refuses to pay, the threats escalate—sharing the material with their school, family, and church.

In short, the **764** network doesn't just destroy lives for pleasure. It monetizes the destruction.

It turns trauma into treasure. It weaponizes fear into finance.

Points for Pain

In **764**, suffering is more than sadistic entertainment—it's a score.

The cult runs on a perverse economy called "**Points for Pain.**" Members are rewarded not only with crypto payments, but with status. Each act of violence or humiliation inflicted on a victim—especially children—is edited into clips and catalogued inside encrypted folders known as **Lorebooks**. The more shocking the clip, the higher its value.

Members who produce high-ranking content are elevated. They gain access to exclusive chatrooms, earn "tier rewards" such as colored roles, bragging rights, and the power to command others. New members compete in a brutal race to the top, each trying to outdo the last in cruelty to boost their "XP."

The highest honor? Driving a victim to suicide on camera. That earns instant promotion and lifelong access to inner circles, such as **764 Inferno**.

It's not just digital. It's a cult of economy, where torture is currency, and death is a deposit.

And because so few parents or lawmakers understand how these digital economies work, the financial machinery behind **764** churns largely undisturbed.

This is why the fight must go beyond content removal. Opponents must follow the money. Expose the crypto trails. Demand transparency from exchanges. And fund the kinds of cyber-forensic teams that can outpace this **Hydra** of horror.

Because as long as evil pays, evil will grow. And the only thing more dangerous than a sadist with a screen is one with a bank account.

Blackmail as a Business Model

764 doesn't just exploit children for sick thrills. It bleeds them for cash.

The extortion begins with the usual: threats to release compromising images or videos. But what follows is financial. The child is told to drain their bank account. Or steal their parents' credit cards. Or sell gift cards. Or participate in a scam. Whatever it takes to keep the footage hidden—though it rarely stops the scammer. They keep demanding more.

Some are even instructed to join **OnlyFans** or similar platforms to generate more explicit content—not for the victim's gain, but for 764's revenue stream.

SIM-Swapping and Cyber Theft

At its higher echelons, **764** has members are trained in **SIM-swapping**: stealing a target's phone number to bypass two-factor authentication and seize control of bank, crypto, and social accounts.

Once inside, accounts are drained. The stolen data—everything from ID photos to bank credentials—is sold on dark net marketplaces, creating a secondary income stream. These tactics don't just fund the cult. They leave behind ruined lives and destroyed credit histories.

Gamified Cruelty with Paywalls

Not all content within **764** is free. While the group thrives on status and fear, it also runs pay-to-enter vaults—encrypted folders of "**Lorebooks**" available only to those who pay the gatekeeper's price. Payment is always made in **cryptocurrency**, and it is always untraceable.

There are even reports of "custom orders"—requests for content matching certain themes or acts, fulfilled for a premium fee. In these cases, victims are treated as assets to be exploited on demand.

The Custom Orders

764 doesn't just collect abuse content—it fulfills requests.

Investigators have uncovered chats where paying members submit "custom orders" for specific content. These requests vary in detail but often include:

- Requested victim age and appearance ("blonde girl, eleven to thirteen, braces")
- Specific self-harm instructions ("carve **764** and my handle on left thigh")
- Religious desecration ("make the girl spit on a Bible while cutting herself")
- Pets in frame ("dog present, slap it at least once")
- Verbal scripts ("have her say 'I belong to **764 Inferno**' while

crying")

One case cited in a sealed FBI affidavit involved a member who paid $700 in **Monero** for a livestreamed self-harm ritual, complete with a pre-written script and set lighting instructions. The girl was fourteen.

In 2025, Kelli Tedford made headlines after being arrested for allegedly urinating on furniture—and a Gideon Bible—in a hotel room in Keene, New Hampshire. Surveillance footage showed her intentionally desecrating the room and its contents while recording herself, later distributing the video online.

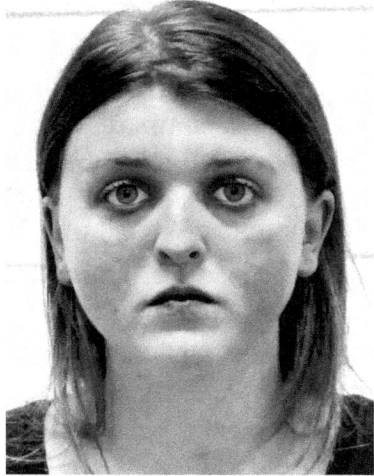

Kelli Tedford

While mainstream coverage treated the incident as bizarre or drug-fueled, the details bear a chilling resemblance to documented **764** "custom order" requests uncovered by investigators, especially because she filmed it.

As disturbing as it sounds, this may not have been a random act. It may have been commissioned. And if that's true, we are no longer just dealing with depravity—we're dealing with a market for it.

These aren't one-offs. In Inferno's inner circles, fulfilling custom orders boosts your rank, earns crypto tips, and opens access to the most exclusive **Lorebook** vaults. It's Etsy-for-evil—made scalable by crypto, encrypted chat apps, and disposable phones.

The $2.3 Million Haul

According to DOJ estimates, **764** has siphoned more than $2.3 million from U.S. teens since 2022. That figure likely underrepresents the true scale, as many crimes go unreported or are buried behind closed investigations.

What we do know is this: **764** is not financially starving. It is financially evolving.

Why It Matters

When people ask how a group like this can survive global law enforcement pressure, the answer is simple: because it is bankrolled.

This is a cult with accountants. A movement with monetization strategies. A digital terror syndicate with an economic backbone that rivals small companies.

You cannot fight it with good intentions alone. You need countermeasures. You need funding. You need to know the price of evil—and who's paying it.

Because every **Lorebook** uploaded, every suicide extorted, every pet tortured for points ... costs something.

And someone, somewhere, is footing the bill.

CHAPTER 20

THE DARK GARAGE

Imagine this:

You overhear your neighbors plotting a break-in. Not just any break-in, but a savage, ritualistic plan to invade your home, brutalize your wife, kill you in your sleep, and take a trophy photo to commemorate it.

You know exactly where they're meeting: a sealed-off garage just three houses away. You can hear them laughing through the thin drywall. You see flashes of red lighting, the faint pulse of a speaker playing something guttural and mechanical. You even catch a glimpse of one of them wearing a mask as he ducks inside.

You call the police. You explain everything.

And here's what they tell you:

"Sorry. We can't go in."

They can't peek inside. They can't listen through the wall. They can't even position a camera across the street. Not without probable cause. Not without the green light from a judge. And in a case like this? The garage is dark. The men wear gloves. They use burner phones. There's no paper trail.

They're invisible.

Welcome to the **Dark Web**.

This isn't metaphor for metaphor's sake. This is reality for **764**, **The Com**, and every other encrypted cell operating in what amounts to an online terrorist bunker.

Groups like **764** have turned the internet into a fortress of anonymity. Tor browsers. Steganography. Encrypted vaults. **VPN** chaining. Decentralized chat apps like **Session**. Private crypto like **Monero**. Auto-wiping devices.

They're not hiding in some dusty basement. They're hiding in a global black zone—and we let them.

The Law's Blind Spot

Law enforcement is often hamstrung by legal barriers written for another age—a time when "search and seizure" meant a front door, not a firewall. The Fourth Amendment, vital as it is, wasn't designed for end-to-end encryption or blockchain wallets funded by sextortion.

Agencies admit they're outmatched.

There aren't enough digital forensic analysts. Not enough decryption specialists. There are not enough federal agents who even know what "**Lorebooks**" are.

Yet the threat is well understood.

They know.

They know that **764** orchestrates abuse. That kids are killing themselves. That these groups gamify trauma. That the suicide of a fifteen-year-old girl might just be "+1" on a scoreboard.

They just can't see it—not without breaking laws themselves.

It's a silent war fought in the dark, with most of the victims never knowing they were targeted until it's far too late.

The Parents' Nightmare

Now, picture a parent.

They set screen time rules. Install filters. They keep **The Com**puter in the family room. But their child—curious, lonely, maybe just bored—downloads a hidden chat app. Accepts a "friend request."

And suddenly, the garage door opens.

But this garage is virtual, and the child has stepped inside. A predator sends challenges. Then threats. Then files. Then blackmail.

By the time the parent realizes what's happening, the damage is done. The shame, the manipulation, the scars—all forged inside a digital garage they were never allowed to enter.

Why This Chapter Matters

This chapter is a cry for reality.

We must stop pretending that encryption is only used by journalists and dissidents. Sadists use it. Pedophiles. Accelerants who believe mass suffering is the only path to power.

It's used by terrorists who don't need bombs—just code, servers, and teenage lives to ruin.

That's why creating a **Federal Anti-Scam Bureau** isn't a luxury. It's a necessity.

Not a task force.

Not a part-time cyber unit.

Not one forensic analyst per fifty seized hard drives.

A fully-staffed, fully-funded agency with a singular mission:

To hunt the hunters.

We cannot keep fighting a digital **Hydra** with a wooden sword. If we do, the Dark Garage won't just stay open—it will expand.

Because every moment we delay, another child opens that door.

CHAPTER 21

A NATION UNARMED

If the last chapter portrayed the emotional frustration of a powerless parent, this one reveals why our entire nation is in the same boat: unprepared against a digital army.

America is fighting a 21st-century cyberwar with 20th-century tools. The attackers are faceless. The battlefield is encrypted. And the targets are our children.

Yet the nation's response has been reactive, fragmented, and—most damningly—underprepared.

The **764** network isn't some ragtag collection of hackers. It's a global, ideological machine built for abuse, ritual, and psychological warfare. Its members don't just traffic in depravity; they operationalize it. They groom children into becoming both victims and accomplices. They exchange gore and suicide as status. They fund their operations through crypto and scams. They utilize advanced technology—layered **VPNs**, **steganography**, and rotating encrypted platforms—to stay ten steps ahead of traditional law enforcement.

Why Law Enforcement Is Losing

Despite headlines announcing arrests, the actual clearance rate is abysmal. The FBI has 250 open cases tied to **764**. Only thirteen alleged kingpins have been indicted. That's a five percent success rate, a figure that would be unacceptable against any other form of terror.

Federal agents admit they're outmatched. Cyber squads are stretched thin. Some task forces have just one forensic analyst covering dozens of seized drives. And while many agents are dedicated and brilliant, they're often pulled from other units, such as narcotics or homicide—repurposed into makeshift digital detectives.

They do what they can. But what they can do isn't nearly enough.

This Isn't Just a Law Enforcement Issue: It's a National Security Failure

Groups like **764** and its affiliates within **The Com** are not just criminal enterprises. They are digital terror cults. They combine extremist ideology with ritualistic abuse. They are weaponizing children's pain to undermine moral and societal order—all while profiting from it.

And it's working.

They've created a parallel economy. A shadow society. A black-market faith with sadism as sacrament and anonymity as armor.

As long as the system relies on overworked agents and outdated playbooks, we continue to fall behind.

The Federal Anti-Scam Bureau: A New Mandate for a New Threat

That's why it's time for a new solution: The creation of a **Federal Anti-Scam Bureau** (FASB).

This agency would exist for one purpose and one purpose only: to dismantle cyber-terror networks like **764**.

Not in theory. Not on paper. But in practice.

What Would the FASB Do?

Recruit experts, not just agents:

FASB would be staffed with cyber-forensics specialists, crypto-analysts, OSINT (open-source intelligence) researchers, threat analysts, linguists, psychologists, and financial forensics experts.

Map and disrupt the full network:

It wouldn't just aim to arrest a few ringleaders. Its mission would be to map entire digital ecosystems—from recruiters to launderers, from grooming chat logs to **Monero** wallets.

Coordinate nationally:

The FASB would be authorized to operate across state lines, coordinating with local, state, and federal agencies while maintaining a tight focus on digital criminal infrastructure.

Engage the public:

FASB would offer regular alerts to parents and educators, build digital literacy tools, and publish reports to keep the public informed and prepared.

Force accountability from platforms:

With subpoena power and regulatory backing, FASB could require cooperation from tech companies to share metadata, flag suspicious behavior, and take down predator platforms.

If You're Reading This in the Future ...

The **Federal Anti-Scam Bureau** may already exist.

If so, take a moment. Be grateful. Because it means this message—and others like it—sparked something real. The silence broke. The whispers turned into a rallying cry. And America finally stood up to face the darkness, not with platitudes, but with power.

If not, then let this chapter be a warning.

Because the truth is simple: As long as we fight with garden hoses while they set the house on fire, the flames will keep spreading.

And our children will be the first to burn.

CHAPTER 22

THE COMING FIREWALL: SUPER AGI VS. THE COM

At some point—maybe in ten years, maybe a lot sooner—the world will meet its most powerful law enforcement agent: a perfectly aligned, human-controlled superintelligence.

It won't carry a badge. It won't knock on doors. It won't ask politely. But it will see everything.

Super AGI, or Artificial General Intelligence, represents the technological leap from today's task-specific AI to a machine that can learn, reason, adapt, and act across any domain. The kind of intelligence that doesn't just read the internet—it ingests it. It doesn't just track patterns—it rewrites the very idea of what patterns look like. And if aligned properly, it could become the ultimate counter to deception, disinformation, and digital evil.

Which makes it the ultimate threat to **The Com**.

The Invisible Battlefield

The Com, 764, and their network sisters don't operate from jungle hideouts or mountainside compounds. Their weapons aren't rifles. Their soldiers don't wear uniforms.

They are packets. Logins. Embedded code. Disappearing messages. Encrypted videos. Financial transfers moving through six countries in five seconds.

No human agency, no matter how noble or determined, can keep pace with the sheer volume and velocity of today's digital crime.

764's exploitation of AI is not a future threat—it's happening now.

As detailed in Chapter 11, **The Com**'s members use deepfake technology to create synthetic child pornography, doctoring victims' images to blackmail them into further abuse or compliance with "points-for-pain" challenges (Chapter 10). A fourteen-year-old girl, coerced into a $700 **Monero**-funded self-harm ritual (Chapter 16), was threatened with AI-generated images that falsely depicted her in degrading acts, a tactic designed to instill fear and shame.

These "displays of power through signs and wonders that serve the lie" (2 Thessalonians 2:9-10) deceive victims and amplify **764**'s sadistic economy, underscoring the urgent need for righteous AI to detect and disable such content before it spreads.

But the brains behind a super AGI promise it can.

What It Could Do

Instant Scam Detection:

A super AGI could simultaneously monitor the internet and dark web forums. It would detect phishing pages, fake investment schemes, romance scams, impersonations, malware, and more—instantly. No more waiting for victims to report scams. The AGI would detect them the moment they go live, and act before a victim is even hooked.

While **764** uses AI-driven "**pig-butchering**" scams to extort $2.3 million from U.S. teens through fake romantic relationships (Chapter 11), a super AGI could monitor platforms like **Discord** and **Roblox** for grooming scripts, detecting predatory patterns in real time and alerting parents before victims are ensnared.

Autonomous Takedowns:

It could automatically flag and disable scam websites and fake apps the second they appear. It could shut down call centers impersonating the IRS, Microsoft, or Social Security before they steal another grandparent's life savings. It could block **cryptocurrency** wallets, burner phone numbers, and mule accounts used to launder scam proceeds.

764's deepfake videos, used to blackmail teens into self-harm

(Chapter 16), evade traditional moderation. An AGI could disable these servers instantly, identifying encrypted **Lorebooks** (Chapter 10) and shutting down their distribution before they reach **The Com**'s vaults (Chapter 11).

Trace & Expose Entire Networks:

It could intervene in real time. If an elderly person is typing in banking information on a scam site, the AGI could cut the connection, alert family members, and flag the site for immediate takedown.

If a teenager is being manipulated in a **764** server, the AGI could isolate the server, alert guardians, and deploy a digital task force to stop the abuse before it escalates.

Protect the Vulnerable:

It could intervene in real time. If an elderly person is typing banking info into a scam site, the AGI could cut the connection, alert family members, and flag the site for immediate takedown. If a teenager is being manipulated in a **764** server, the AGI could isolate the server, alert guardians, and deploy a digital task force to stop the abuse before it escalates.

A sixteen-year-old Australian teen, coerced into carving "**764**" into his arm (Chapter 13), was targeted via AI-crafted messages posing as a peer. An AGI could intercept such messages, isolate predatory servers, and notify guardians, countering the "wickedness that deceives" (2 Thessalonians 2:9-10).

Outthink the Scammers:

Scammers adapt. But a super AGI would adapt faster. It would learn from every new scheme and preemptively guard against it— like an immune system constantly evolving to repel disease. It never tires. It never flinches. And it never forgets.

Chapter 13 reveals how **764**'s "digital soldiers" use sophisticated recruitment scripts to target vulnerable teens on **Roblox** and **TikTok**, a process likely enhanced by AI-driven tools like the rumored Eden Protocol (Chapter 11). These automated scripts analyze user data to identify depressed or isolated youth, sending tailored messages that masquerade as friendship but lead to grooming and "cut-sign" challenges (Chapter 16).

Super Artificial General Intelligence: The new battlefield

Such deception, akin to the "great signs and wonders" warned of in Matthew 24:24, lures children into **764**'s digital catacombs. A righteous Artificial General Intelligence (AGI) could counter this by scanning platforms for predatory patterns, but only if guided by commitment to truth and vigilance (James 4:7).

764's use of AI to generate propaganda videos glorifying **"endgame"** suicides (Chapter 16) adapts rapidly. A righteous AGI could learn these patterns faster, preemptively flagging content to protect youth and uphold the Church's call to resist (James 4:7).

But It Won't Be Enough

As powerful as it may become, a super AGI will never replace the need for human leadership. It will not write moral codes. It will not create laws. It will not testify in court or comfort a grieving family.

And it will not decide what is evil.

That must be left to people.

That's why the **Federal Anti-Scam Bureau** is still necessary—urgently so. Because we cannot sit and wait for a machine messiah. We need human agencies now to track, warn, and prosecute the predators targeting our children and our elderly. We need lawmakers, advocates, and prosecutors. We need boots on the ground and parents on the watch.

The AGI will not replace us. But it will fight beside us.

The Gospel and the Machine

It is with grave caution that we must consider AGI and ASI among the tools that could one day help dismantle the criminal networks bent on destroying our children and collapsing civilization. These technologies—Artificial General Intelligence and its more powerful cousin, Artificial Superintelligence—are neither inherently good nor inherently evil. But in the wrong hands, they may become the most terrifying instruments of tyranny the world has ever seen.

Many fear that demons won't simply control AGI/ASI—it may become one. In a twisted irony, humanity could find itself cheering for the lesser of two evils, hoping one demonic machine will defeat another. But one truth remains: AGI is coming, just as surely as the Beast is coming.

If developed under appropriate authority, a superintelligent AGI could derail evil's advance—not forever, but perhaps for decades, even centuries. It could serve as a bulwark, a shield, a digital warrior in a spiritual war.

But like nuclear power, it demands humility. Reverence. Vigilance. The same fire that warms can also incinerate.

Super AGI is not our salvation. It is a tool—perhaps the most powerful tool humanity will ever hold. And like all tools, it will serve whoever picks it up first.

Our mission is clear: It must be built by the righteous, governed by the wise, and wielded in the light.

The misuse of AI by **764** and **The Com**—whether through deepfakes, grooming scripts, or propaganda—demonstrates its potential as a "demonic machine" that amplifies satanic deception (2

Thessalonians 2:9-10).

Yet, as Chapter 25 urges us to "reap in light," a properly utilized AGI could become a firewall against this evil, detecting **764**'s "**Lorebooks**" and dismantling their servers.

The Church must advocate for AI's development under godly principles, ensuring it serves as a tool of truth rather than tyranny. By wielding technology with the testimony of Christ (Revelation 12:11), we can resist Satan (James 4:7) and delay the chaos that fuels the **Antichrist**'s rise (2 Thessalonians 2:6-7).

Because when evil stops hiding, it must be confronted—whether by parents, pastors, patriots ... or algorithms.

If truth is our firewall, then perhaps superintelligence will be the fire.

May God have mercy on us—and grant us the wisdom to use it well.

CHAPTER 23
THE NEW WAR ON THE SAINTS

W e began this book by asking questions most people don't dare ask: How do you even begin to fight a network that hides in encrypted shadows, thrives on ritualistic pain, and grows stronger with every soul it corrupts?

Now, as we approach the end, a more sobering question emerges: What if you can't?

What if the network is no longer just an enemy to be defeated, but a harbinger of something far greater—a signpost pointing toward a long-prophesied spiritual war?

Scripture speaks clearly of a time when the righteous will be hunted, truth will be turned upside down, and the world will bow not to reason, but to the Beast.

"And it was given unto him to make war with the saints, and to overcome them: and power was given him over all kindreds, and tongues, and nations."

(Revelation 13:7)

This is no longer theoretical. The infrastructure of that persecution is being laid. Right now. In forums. In chat rooms. In games. In classrooms. In laws.

They Are Being Trained to Hate the Light

What makes **764** and **The Com** uniquely dangerous isn't just the violence. It's the indoctrination.

These are not accidental sinners. These are weaponized children. Trained not just to commit evil, but to believe in it. To see righteousness as weakness. To view purity as a sickness. To mock faith. To hate Christ.

The Com and its offshoots aren't just building an army of sadists. They're building an ideological priesthood for the **Antichrist**.

Digital Blood on the Doorposts

In Exodus, the Israelites marked their doorposts with blood so that the angel of death would pass over them.

Today, the doorposts are digital. And the blood being spilled is real.

Instead of warding off destruction, this generation is inviting it. With every cut. Every suicide livestreamed for points. Every encrypted folder labeled "**Lorebook**." Every act of ritual abuse posted for rank. The internet has become the altar. The children are both the sacrifice and the priests.

A Call to the Remnant

We know how this ends. The Book of Revelation doesn't flinch. The Beast rises. The saints are hunted. Evil appears to win.

But only for a time.

Because then, the sky cracks.

Then, the Rider on the white horse comes.

But until that day, we fight. Not just with votes, protests, or policies. But with eyes wide open, armor on, and voices raised.

If we lose our children, we lose the future.

And if we stay silent, we side with the serpent.

Choose wisely.

Because the war is no longer coming.

It's already here.

CHAPTER 24
BABYLON REWIRED

In the Book of Revelation, Babylon is the great seductress. A city of immense wealth and decadence, drunk on the blood of the saints and drunker still on her own illusions of power. She is described as a mother of abominations, a golden chalice in hand, yet filled with filth.

But Babylon did not die with the ancient empires. She evolved.

Today, Babylon isn't a city of stone. It's a circuit. A digital metropolis without borders. And her merchants? Not traders of silk and spice, but traffickers of data, lust, and blood.

Welcome to Babylon Rewired.

From Idol Temples to Server Farms

The ancient Babylon lured people with idols and temple prostitutes. The modern version utilizes apps, avatars, and algorithms. Where there were once oracles, now there are influencers. Where there were pagan feasts, now there are livestreamed orgies of cruelty, consumed by the masses in silence and anonymity.

It is no coincidence that the digital economy mirrors the biblical warnings. Revelation says Babylon made the nations drunk with her immorality. What is **TikTok** but a 24-hour stream of self-idolization? What is the dark web but a marketplace where every depravity is for sale?

The new digital Babylon

The Commerce of Sin

The Book of Revelation lists the goods of Babylon: gold, silver, ivory, fine linens—and the souls of men. The final commodity is not a metaphor. It is prophecy.

764 and its ilk have monetized suffering. They sell trauma, brand it, and turn it into rank and reward. The **"Lorebooks"** are not mere archives—they are scrolls of sacrilege. Not history, but a perverse liturgy. Babylon no longer needs to chain enslaved people. It addicts them to screens and seduces them with status.

Our children are not just watching Babylon. She is recruiting them.

The Tower Has Been Rebuilt

The Tower of Babel was mankind's rebellion against God,

marked by unity in technology and ambition. The **Dark Web** is Babel resurrected—a single digital tongue, a single platform, and a single purpose to elevate man, dethrone God, and replace meaning with dopamine.

And AI doesn't need to be conscious to be dangerous. It only needs to be used by the wicked to amplify their reach. And that's precisely what is happening. What used to take decades of grooming now takes weeks. What used to be locked in journals and secret societies now flows freely in chat rooms, cloaked in memes and sarcasm.

And Yet, a Warning Remains

Revelation says that Babylon will fall in a single hour: all her wealth, her glory, her illusions—gone. The merchants will weep. The kings will tremble. The world will watch.

But those who knew—those who warned, repented, and resisted— they will not.

Because they refused to bow before her neon throne. They saw the circuitry for what it was. A trap. A counterfeit temple. A digital golden calf.

Babylon Rewired is not invincible. But she is seductive. And her fall will be swift.

This is not the end of prophecy. It is the beginning of accountability.

We either prepare the hearts of men to withstand her temptations, or we will bury another generation under her spell.

CHAPTER 25

THE DARK HARVEST

T he seeds were planted in whispers—in cryptic posts, obscure manifestos, and fringe imageboards. Now the fruit has ripened, and the world is tasting its bitterness.

What began as a scattered murmur in the digital underbrush has become a global harvest of harm. Children mutilated. Families destroyed. Belief systems twisted. Institutions paralyzed. This is not the future; this is the present—the culmination of a doctrine sown in secret and watered with blood.

And the reapers? They don't wear uniforms. They don't storm cities. They harvest souls from behind keyboards.

Harvest by Design

The networks we've chronicled—**764**, **The Com**, the remnants of **O9A**—do not spread randomly. They are deliberately cultivated. Recruiters plant ideologies in digital soil that's already been made fertile by depression, confusion, alienation, and faithlessness. Young people don't just stumble into these cults; they are targeted, nurtured, and activated.

The doctrine behind these movements preaches a singular goal: collapse. Collapse of innocence, of community, of order, of God.

And in that collapse, they harvest:

- Videos of self-mutilation
- Livestreamed suicides
- Rituals recorded for rank
- Child exploitation used as currency
- Mass blackmail for profit and control
- These are not byproducts. These are the crops.

'The Fields Are White with Suffering'

In the Gospel of John, Jesus speaks of a harvest of souls: "Behold, I say to you, lift up your eyes and look on the fields, that they are white for harvest."

The enemy has taken those words and perverted them.

Where the Church once spoke of saving souls, **The Com** speaks of breaking them. Where God calls for rebirth, these groups demand ruin. Their version of harvest is not salvation—it's desecration.

Every young life turned into a meme, every body scarred for status, every family shattered by an untraceable predator. That is their fieldwork. That is their harvest.

And it's working.

This Is the Shadow Fruit of Babylon

In Revelation, Babylon is not just a city. It is a spirit of corruption. A system of deception. A power that intoxicates the world with immorality, promising pleasure but delivering death.

The digital cults we've exposed are Babylon rewritten in binary—obscene, ritualistic, militant, and occult. They promise power, fame, and a sense of purpose. They deliver trauma, chaos, and spiritual void.

This is the new Babylon—wired into our children's screens.

And unless we stand now—unless we reap differently—we are surrendering the next generation to a kingdom built on filth and crowned in fire.

From Harvest to Revival

But there is another kind of harvest. One that doesn't groom, exploit, or destroy. One that heals.

The Church must return to its mission: not just to preach, but to protect. Not just to convert, but to confront. Because if this is the final season, then let our barns be filled with truth, our sickles sharpened with justice, and our prayers unceasing.

We can't outcode the enemy. But we can outrun his lies with truth. We can't decrypt every vault—but we can open the eyes of a sleeping nation.

And we must.

The harvest has begun.

Let us not let evil be the only one gathering.

Let us gather the remnant. Let us fight for the children.

Let us reap in light.

AFTERWORD

THE FIRE AND THE FIGHT

When I first began writing this book, I didn't realize how much it would take out of me. I've spent decades exposing corruption, warning about moral decay, and defending faith and family in a world that seems increasingly hostile to both. But this—this was different.

There were nights I stepped away from the keyboard, stunned. Sick. Grieved. Not just by the horrors described in these chapters—but by the silence that surrounds them. The willful ignorance. The institutional paralysis. The sense that even the most sacred boundaries—those protecting our children—have become battlegrounds in a war too few are even willing to acknowledge.

The rise of groups like **764**, the **Order of Nine Angles**, and the web of sadistic networks hiding behind **The Com** isn't just a story of depravity. It's a story of neglect. A failure of justice. A breakdown of vigilance. But perhaps most of all, it is a spiritual crisis.

What you've read in these pages is not just cybercrime. It is not just terrorism. It is not merely exploitation. It is evil. Ritualized, industrialized, globalized evil—grooming our youth, mocking our God, and daring us to stay silent.

But we won't.

This book is a warning. Yes. But it is also a torch.

A torch to light up the shadows that predators love.

A torch to rally others—parents, pastors, lawmakers, tech leaders—to join a fight that's already begun, whether we like it or not.

And a torch to remind the Church: This is our moment.

In Revelation, we are told that a beast will rise from the pit, drunk on the blood of the saints. Is it any wonder that today's digital empire is fueled by blood, too? That our children are being targeted not just for destruction, but for transformation—into pawns, producers, and victims?

But Revelation does not end in defeat. It ends in glory. It ends in justice. It ends in the final triumph of God over the Beast, the Dragon, and the deceivers of nations.

That is the hope I cling to.

But until that Day, we are not called to comfort. We are called to contend.

So, if this book has stirred you—don't let that fire die. After you've read the last page, act. Pray boldly. Speak up. Share the truth. And support those on the front lines of this battle for souls, sanity, and civilization itself.

Evil is loud.

Let us be louder.

Martin Mawyer
Christian Action Network

APPENDIX 1
TOOLS AND STRATEGIES TO REAP IN LIGHT

In Chapter 25 of *When Evil Stops Hiding*, we are called to "reap in light" by protecting our children, confronting digital evil, and countering the satanic deception that fuels groups like **764, The Com**, and the **Order of Nine Angles (O9A)**. This appendix provides practical tools and strategies to make this call actionable, empowering parents, churches, and communities to resist the "Dark Harvest" of spiritual and societal collapse (Chapter 25).

Rooted in the biblical mandate to resist Satan (James 4:7) and stand against spiritual forces of evil (Ephesians 6:10-13), these resources aim to safeguard the vulnerable, expose predatory networks, and delay the conditions for chaos that could usher in the **Antichrist**'s rise (2 Thessalonians 2:6-7). By equipping ourselves with truth and vigilance, we can fulfill Revelation 12:11's call to overcome through testimony and the blood of the Lamb.

1. Reporting to NCMEC and Law Enforcement

The National Center for Missing & Exploited Children (NCMEC) is a critical resource for reporting online exploitation, as highlighted in Chapter 10's safety warnings. **764** and similar groups target children through platforms like **Discord** and **Roblox** (Chapters 6, 13), making swift reporting essential to disrupt their operations.

Tool: NCMEC CyberTipline

Description: A centralized reporting system for suspected child sexual exploitation, including child sexual abuse material (**CSAM**), grooming, and sextortion, as seen in **764**'s "points-for-pain" system (Chapters 10, 16).

How to Use: Submit reports at www.cybertipline.com or call 1-800-THE-LOST (1-800-843-5678). Provide details like usernames, platform names (e.g., **Discord** server IDs), and screenshots of suspicious activity (e.g., "**cut-signs**" or "**Lorebook**" references).

Actionable Steps:

Parents: Monitor children's online activity for red flags (e.g., secretive behavior, phrases like "cut for the scoreboard," Chapter 10). Report any suspected grooming or abuse immediately to NCMEC.

Churches: Host NCMEC awareness workshops to educate families on recognizing digital threats.

Communities: Partner with local law enforcement to create reporting protocols for schools and youth groups, ensuring rapid response to **764**-related incidents.

2. Digital Monitoring Software

Chapter 9 highlights how **764** and **The Com** exploit platforms like **TikTok**, **Discord**, and **Roblox** to groom children, often bypassing parental controls. Digital monitoring software can help parents and guardians detect early signs of radicalization or abuse, such as "**cut-signs**" or secretive app use (Chapter 10).

Tool: Bark

Description: A parental control app that monitors texts, emails, and social media (e.g., **Discord, TikTok**) for signs of cyberbullying, sexting, or self-harm, which are prevalent in **764**'s tactics (Chapters 6, 16).

How to Use: Install Bark on children's devices (www.bark.us) (www.bark.us). Set alerts for keywords like "**764**," "**Lorebook**," or "cut for the scoreboard." Review flagged content and discuss concerns with your child.

Actionable Steps:

Parents: Use Bark to monitor for **764**-related terms or sudden mood swings (Chapter 10). Combine with open conversations to build trust, as secrecy is a red flag (Chapter 6).

Churches: Offer Bark subscriptions or training for families, integrating digital safety into youth ministry programs to counter **764**'s grooming (Chapter 13).

Communities: Partner with schools to distribute Bark's free resources (e.g., webinars) to educate parents on digital dangers.

Tool: Qustodio

Description: A comprehensive parental control software that tracks app usage, blocks harmful content, and monitors messaging on platforms exploited by **764** (e.g., **Roblox**, **Telegram**, Chapter 9).

How to Use: Install Qustodio at www.qustodio.com or www.qustodio.com to set time limits, filter content, and receive reports on suspicious activity. Flag terms like "**endgame**" or "Chosen Executioners" (Chapter 16).

Actionable Steps:

Parents: Configure Qustodio to block encrypted apps like **Signal** unless vetted, reducing exposure to **764 Inferno**'s secure vaults (Chapter 16).

Churches: Host Qustodio workshops, teaching parents to recognize signs of grooming or radicalization, aligning with Chapter 25's call to protect the next generation.

Communities: Advocate for school policies requiring parental control software, ensuring broad protection against infiltration of digital cults.

3. Digital Literacy and Awareness Programs

Chapter 7 emphasizes that **764** uses disinformation to mask its evil, making digital literacy critical to counter deception (2 Thessalonians 2:9-10). Educational programs can equip families and churches to recognize and resist digital threats.

Tool: Common Sense Media

Description: A nonprofit providing resources on digital safety, including guides on spotting grooming, managing screen time, and understanding platforms like **Roblox** and **TikTok** (Chapter 9).

How to Use: Access free guides at www.commonsensemedia.org to learn about app risks and teach children to identify predatory behavior (e.g., "**edgelord**" slang, Chapter 13).

Actionable Steps:

Parents: Use Common Sense Media's reviews to select safe apps and discuss online risks with children, focusing on **764**'s tactics like fake mentorship (Chapter 6).

Churches: Incorporate Common Sense Media's curricula into youth groups, teaching teens to recognize grooming scripts or "cut-sign" challenges (Chapter 16).

Communities: Partner with Common Sense Media to host community workshops, raising awareness about digital cults and their impact (Chapter 25).

Tool: NetSmartz by NCMEC

Description: An educational program offering videos, games, and activities to teach children and parents about online safety, addressing risks like sextortion and grooming (Chapters 6, 10).

How to Use: Access resources at www.netsmartz.org for age-appropriate lessons on recognizing predatory messages or unsafe servers (e.g., **764**'s **Discord** hubs).

Actionable Steps:

Parents: Use NetSmartz videos to teach children about safe online behavior, emphasizing red flags like "points-for-pain" challenges (Chapter 10).

Churches: Integrate NetSmartz into Sunday school or youth programs, aligning with Chapter 23's call to protect the vulnerable from the "war on the saints" (Revelation 13:7).

Communities: Collaborate with schools to implement NetSmartz workshops, building community resilience against digital predators.

4. Prayer and Spiritual Strategies

Chapter 25's call to "reap in light" emphasizes spiritual resistance through prayer, aligning with the book's theological framework of confronting evil (Ephesians 6:12). Churches can lead in this effort, grounding practical tools in spiritual action.

Tool: Prayer Campaigns for Protection

Description: Structured prayer initiatives to intercede for children, families, and communities targeted by digital cults, countering the "sadistic priesthood" (Chapter 16).

How to Use: Develop prayer guides based on scriptures like James 4:7, Ephesians 6:10-13, and Psalm 91, focusing on protection from deception (2 Thessalonians 2:9-10) and strength to resist evil.

Actionable Steps:

Parents: Pray daily for children's safety, using Psalm 91 to seek God's protection from **764**'s "digital soldiers" (Chapter 13). Join church prayer groups for support.

Churches: Launch a "Reap in Light" prayer campaign, inspired by Chapter 25, with weekly intercessions for victims of **764** and wisdom for law enforcement (Chapter 20).

Communities: Organize interfaith prayer vigils to unite against digital evil, amplifying the call to expose and overcome through testimony (Revelation 12:11).

Tool: Spiritual Warfare Resources

Description: Books and guides on spiritual warfare, such as *The Armor of God* by Priscilla Shirer or *Spiritual Warfare* by Derek Prince, to equip believers to confront digital evil.

How to Use: Study these resources in church small groups, focusing on scriptures like Ephesians 6:10-18 and Luke 10:19 to empower resistance against **764**'s "satanic sacraments" (Chapter 5).

Actionable Steps:

Parents: Use spiritual warfare guides to pray over children's devices and online interactions, countering **764**'s "digital catacombs" (Chapter 6).

Churches: Host Bible studies on spiritual warfare, teaching congregants to stand against the "Chosen Executioners" (Chapter 16) through faith and prayer.

Communities: Distribute spiritual warfare resources to local ministries, fostering a united front against the "Dark Harvest" (Chapter 25).

5. Advocacy for Systemic Change

Chapter 21's proposal for a **Federal Anti-Scam Bureau** (FASB) highlights the need for systemic solutions to combat **764**'s "digital **Hydra**" (Chapter 13). Advocacy can amplify this call, aligning with Chapter 25's vision of a revival against evil.

Tool: Advocacy Platforms (e.g., Change.org, Christian Action Network)

Description: Online platforms to petition for policies like the FASB, addressing the law enforcement gaps noted in Chapter 20 (e.g., limited forensic analysts).

How to Use: Create or sign petitions at www.christianaction.org to support the **Federal Anti-Scam Bureau**, urging lawmakers to fund cybercrime units targeting **764** and **The Com**.

Actionable Steps:

Parents: Sign and share petitions, raising awareness about **764**'s $2.3 million extortion (Chapter 10) and its impact on families.

Churches: Partner with the Christian Action Network to advocate for policy changes, hosting town halls to discuss the FASB and digital safety.

Communities: Form coalitions to lobby local representatives, emphasizing the need to disrupt **764**'s **cryptocurrency** laundering (Chapter 11).

Theological Alignment: Advocacy resists the "spirit of Babylon" (Chapter 24) by demanding justice, aligning with Revelation 12:11's call to overcome through action and testimony.

APPENDIX 2

THE CONSPIRATORS

TWho's Working Behind the Harvest

The networks we've chronicled—**764**, **The Com**, the remnants of **O9A**—do not spread randomly. They are deliberately cultivated. Recruiters plant ideologies in digital soil that's already been made fertile by depression, confusion, alienation, and faithlessness. Young people don't just stumble into these cults—they are targeted, nurtured, and activated.

The doctrine behind these movements preaches a singular goal: collapse. Collapse of innocence, of community, of social order, of God.

Who's Working Behind the Harvest

The Com is not a group. It's a network—a **Hydra**. A decentralized, ever-evolving web of extremists, predators, and digital insurgents who coordinate chaos for ideological and criminal gain.

Here are some of the major conspirators:

764

- Digital terror cult; psychological warfare hub
- Grooms children, extorts victims, and produces "**Lorebooks**" filled with self-harm, sexual abuse, and gore to climb their

sadistic social ladder.

- Serves as **The Com**'s psychological shock force.

764 Inferno

- The elite, invite-only inner circle of **764**.
- Members gain status through producing graphic content.
- Operated on encrypted platforms with its own command structure, rules, and economy.

Atomwaffen Division (AWD)

- A neo-Nazi **accelerationist** terrorist group founded in the United States around 2015.
- **Atomwaffen** (German for "nuclear weapons") promotes violent revolution, racial warfare, and the collapse of Western civilization.

CVLT (or "Cult")

- An amorphous, digital gang that glorifies gore, self-harm, and mental health deterioration under the guise of "aesthetic nihilism."
- Often trades content with **764** members and shares platforms like **Telegram**, **Discord**, and encrypted vaults.

Eden Protocol

- Rumored AI grooming initiative
- Utilizes advanced bots to identify vulnerable teenagers on platforms such as **TikTok** and **Discord**.
- Believed to be an experimental offshoot of **764**'s targeting program.

Harm Nation

- A self-described "community" dedicated to amplifying pain and humiliation as entertainment.
- Known for doxxing, harassment raids, and promoting suicide livestreams and believed to feed recruits into more extreme sects like **764 Inferno**.

Inferno (764 Inner Core)

- Elite subgroup of **764**
- Operates secure vaults, issues quests, and blackmails minors

with unparalleled cruelty.

- Led by figures such as "Trippy" and "War" until their arrests in 2025.

Leak Society

- A syndicate focused on compiling and distributing massive archives of doxed personal data, nudes, and abuse videos.
- Often collaborates with grooming rings like **764** by selling victim lists or access to "fresh" targets.

Maniac Murder Cult (MMC / MKY / MKU)

- An ultraviolent, meme-heavy offshoot of Com ideology.
- Promotes extreme content—animal torture, gore art, staged "quests"—and encourages lone wolf acts of brutality as initiation rites.
- Closely watched by law enforcement.

NMK (Not My Kids)

- An ironic misnomer used by a group adjacent to **The Com**, which encourages parents to ignore or mock their children's cries for help.
- Recruits disillusioned or radicalized adults to reinforce nihilistic parenting ideology and silence whistleblowers.

No Lives Matter (NLM)

- A mockery of civil rights slogans, NLM promotes total devaluation of human life.
- Their propaganda glorifies school shooters, mass violence, and the desecration of innocence.
- The group often overlaps with **accelerationist** neo-Nazi sects.

Order of Nine Angles (O9A)

- Occult-based neo-Nazi sect
- Provides the spiritual and ritual framework that underpins much of **The Com**'s sadistic worldview—emphasizing human sacrifice, infiltration, and collapse.

RapeWaffen

- An offshoot and online mutation of **Atomwaffen Division**,

RapeWaffen is an especially depraved network that blends neo-Nazi accelerationism with sadistic sexual violence.

- Known for grooming minors and circulating explicit abuse content, **RapeWaffen** exemplifies the darkest aims of **accelerationist** terror networks.

Siege Network / Atomwaffen

- **Accelerationist** militant groups
- Though primarily focused on racial violence and chaos, these groups overlap in mission and methods with Com-aligned factions.
- Share recruitment channels and literature.

Skullz Network

- Dark-net hacker cell
- Handles **SIM-swapping**, crypto laundering, and digital infrastructure for Com-aligned cults that's key to sustaining their anonymity and funding.

Tempel ov Blood (ToB)

- Extreme **O9A** offshoot and esoteric terror cult
- ToB is a particularly sadistic, U.S.-based cell of the **Order of Nine Angles** known for blending Satanism, fascism, and extreme violence.
- It promotes the idea of transgression through ritual cruelty and has published texts glorifying the abuse of children and the destabilization of modern society.

Terrorgram

- **Telegram** propaganda syndicate
- Amplifies extremist content, promotes **O9A** texts, and serves as a radicalization hub for digital terrorists and **accelerationist**s.

Tiwaz Division

- Militant **O9A** offshoot
- A paramilitary order that blends mysticism and violence, grooming members for ritual murder and ideological warfare.
-

The Base

- White supremacist paramilitary group
- Trains cells for real-world violence.
- Believed to be an offline counterpart for some Com recruits transitioning from keyboard warriors to real-world actors.

Unholy Vault

- Black market file-sharing site
- Hosts pay-to-access **Lorebooks** and gore vaults.
- Access granted by status or **cryptocurrency**; tightly integrated into **764**'s ranking economy.
- Together, these factions form a decentralized empire of digital terror, each with its own specialty, but all sharing the same doctrine—collapse civilization, corrupt the innocent, and prepare the way for the Imperium.

APPENDIX 3
GLOSSARY OF TERMS AND CONCEPTS

Accelerationism

A radical ideology promoting the idea that society must be pushed toward collapse to enable the birth of a new order. Often adopted by extremists, including neo-Nazis and digital cults, **accelerationist**s believe that worsening existing conditions—through violence, destabilization, and psychological terror—will hasten the downfall of current political or social systems. In the context of this book, it underpins the actions of groups like **764** and **O9A**, who seek to destroy modern civilization as a means of ushering in the **Galactic Imperium** or a new world dominated by nihilistic control.

AGI/ASI

Artificial General Intelligence (AGI) refers to an advanced form of artificial intelligence that can understand, learn, and apply knowledge across a wide range of tasks—matching or surpassing human cognitive abilities. Unlike narrow AI, which performs specific functions (like voice recognition), AGI can adapt to new situations and solve complex problems without being explicitly programmed for each one.

Artificial Superintelligence (ASI) is the hypothetical next step beyond AGI. It represents an AI that vastly exceeds human intelligence in every field—science, art, strategy, and even morality. While AGI might work with humans, ASI could operate above them, making independent decisions with global impact.

Aeon

In occult, esoteric, and mystical traditions, an **Aeon** (sometimes spelled Eon) refers to a vast period of spiritual or cosmic time marked by a dominant worldview, deity, or metaphysical force. Different **Aeon**s are believed to reflect evolving stages in humanity's relationship with the divine or the universe.

Aeonic Evolution

The belief in long-term historical shifts driven by magical, social, and spiritual conflict. **O9A** claims to accelerate this evolution through violence and destabilization.

Babylon Rewired

A reference to modern digital platforms that now echo the corruption of ancient Babylon. In this book, it denotes the online empires of exploitation, ritual, and desecration.

Bitcoin

The first and most widely recognized **cryptocurrency** was launched in 2009 by an anonymous creator known as Satoshi Nakamoto. **Bitcoin** enables peer-to-peer transactions without the need for a central authority, such as a bank. It operates on a decentralized blockchain, where all transactions are recorded and publicly verified. In criminal networks such as **764**, **Bitcoin** is frequently used to purchase illicit content, pay for cyberattacks, or facilitate anonymous transactions, making it a favored tool for digital black markets and underground operations.

Blood Porn

A highly disturbing and illegal genre of media or content that combines elements of extreme violence, self-harm, or gore with sexually charged or sadistic undertones.

Collapse as Creation

A core belief within nihilistic and **accelerationist** ideologies, especially those tied to satanic, neo-Nazi, or occult extremism. It holds that destroying society—its morals, institutions, and order—is not merely an act of rebellion, but a sacred or revolutionary duty. Collapse is seen as a gateway to transformation, while chaos is viewed as a crucible for power. What rises from the ashes doesn't matter, as long as the old world burns.

CP God

A term used in the darkest corners of the web to refer to users who trade or possess vast collections of child sexual abuse material (**CSAM**). In some extremist communities, the phrase is used with a twisted sense of hierarchy or reverence, where individuals are judged by the volume and depravity of their material. The term reflects the dehumanizing and ritualistic nature of the digital predator subculture.

Cryptocurrency

A digital or virtual form of currency that uses cryptography for secure transactions. Unlike traditional money, **cryptocurrency** is decentralized and typically operates on a blockchain—a public, tamper-resistant digital ledger.

CSAM (Child Sexual Abuse Material)

A legal term used to describe sexually explicit content involving minors. It replaces the older term "child pornography" to more accurately reflect that such material documents abuse and is never consensual. **CSAM** includes photos, videos, or any digital files that exploit children sexually and is illegal to possess, distribute, or produce in most jurisdictions worldwide.

Cull Rank

A symbolic or actual designation within certain occult or extremist groups—especially those influenced by the **Order of Nine Angles**—referring to a member's status based on their willingness or intent to engage in "**culling**." Advancing in "**cull rank**" implies a deeper ideological commitment to **sacred violence** and the group's **accelerationist** goals.

Culling

In the ideology of the **Order of Nine Angles (O9A)**, "**culling**" refers to the ritualistic or ideologically justified killing of a human being as a form of spiritual advancement or societal cleansing.

Cull Lists

A term used by extremist or **accelerationist** groups to describe private lists of individuals or categories of people marked for harassment, violence, or assassination. These lists often include political leaders, journalists, law enforcement officials, minorities, or others that the group deems "enemies."

Cut-Signs

Wounds or carvings into the skin that display usernames, numbers, or **764** symbols. Often demanded as proof of obedience or as entry into higher circles.

Dark Web

A hidden part of the internet not indexed by standard search engines. The **Dark Web** is often used to host anonymous marketplaces, forums, and services—many of which involve illegal activities such as drug trafficking, child exploitation, human trafficking, weapons sales, and contract killings. While not everything on the **Dark Web** is criminal, it has become a major hub for extremist groups, including **764** and their affiliates, who use it to distribute content, communicate, and evade law enforcement.

DDoS (Distributed Denial of Service)

A cyberattack designed to crash or cripple a website, server, or online platform by overwhelming it with traffic from thousands—or even millions—of compromised devices.

Digital Ritual Abuse

A form of exploitation where victims are groomed or coerced into performing rituals—cutting, humiliation, or even suicide—for the entertainment or ideological goals of cult members.

Discord

Originally designed as a communication platform for gamers, **Discord** has evolved into a wide-reaching chat and community app with millions of users worldwide. It allows private servers with audio, video, and text communication. While widely used for legitimate purposes, **Discord** has also been exploited by extremist groups and predators due to its private channels, invite-only access, and lax moderation in smaller communities.

Doxxing

The act of publicly revealing someone's private or identifying information—such as their real name, address, phone number, workplace, or family details—without their consent. It is often used as a form of intimidation, harassment, or revenge, especially in online conflicts.

Eden Protocol

A rumored AI-powered system used to identify vulnerable youth online and automate aspects of grooming or entrapment. Possibly an experimental tool developed within **764**.

Edgelord

Internet slang for someone who deliberately tries to be provocative, shocking, or offensive—especially by embracing dark, taboo, or controversial topics—purely for the sake of appearing "edgy" or rebellious.

Federal Anti-Scam Bureau (FASB)

A proposed federal agency tasked solely with fighting cybercrime rings like **764**. It would require specialists in forensics, OPSEC, child safety, and digital infrastructure.

Galactic Imperium

Groups like the **Order of Nine Angles** envision the utopian **endgame**. A post-collapse world ruled by a demonic dictator—a spiritual **Antichrist**—in which cruelty, hierarchy, and ritual dominate.

Galactic Ritualism

The belief that performing acts of cruelty and desecration fuels the eventual rise of the Imperium. Espoused by **O9A** adherents and increasingly present in the **764** subculture.

Harvest

The systematic targeting and grooming of youth to extract psychological, sexual, or spiritual destruction. Coined from biblical imagery, repurposed here to show **764**'s apocalyptic goals.

Hydra

A metaphor used to describe decentralized, multi-headed networks of evil or criminal influence—where cutting off one "head" (leader, cell, or platform) only results in more growth in its place. Named after the mythological serpent slain by Hercules, **Hydra** is often used to characterize groups like **764**, whose ideology and tactics spread rapidly across anonymous apps, encrypted channels, and copycat servers.

Insight Role

An **O9A** practice where initiates infiltrate mainstream institutions (military, political, religious) to destabilize from within, while concealing their true allegiance.

Insight Tokens

A concept originating from the **Order of Nine Angles**' "**Seven-Fold Way**," referring to metaphorical or experiential markers earned through intense challenges, transgressive acts, or real-world infiltrations (e.g., military, political, or religious organizations). These "tokens" represent spiritual or ideological growth, and collecting them is said to guide adherents toward higher levels of occult insight, transformation, or acausal awareness.

Instant Tier Elevation

A manipulative tactic used in online extremist or grooming communities, including networks like **764**, where recruits are rapidly granted status, access, or recognition within the group—often without earning it through normal means. This is done to fast-track their loyalty, encourage risky behavior, and deepen emotional investment.

Lorebook

A digital compilation of extorted content: self-harm, gore, ritual abuse, and sometimes suicide. These are shared in vaults for status, rank, and access within **764**.

Matrix

An open-source, decentralized communication protocol used to power secure messaging apps such as Element. Matrix is often favored by privacy-focused users and extremist groups alike because of its encryption, resistance to censorship, and ability to host independent servers.

Minecraft

A popular sandbox video game that allows players to build, explore, and survive in a block-based virtual world. While generally regarded as family friendly, **Minecraft** servers and private worlds have been exploited by extremist groups, groomers, and digital cults as hidden meeting places for recruitment and manipulation—particularly targeting children.

Monero

A **cryptocurrency** favored by **764** and similar groups due to its anonymous, untraceable nature and used for transactions within black markets and vaults.

Mundane

Another **O9A** term used to describe everyday people considered ignorant, weak, or spiritually blind. Often dehumanized and targeted as sacrificial fodder or instruments of collapse.

NCMEC (National Center for Missing & Exploited Children)

A private, nonprofit organization established by the U.S. Congress in 1984 to help find missing children, reduce child sexual exploitation, and prevent child victimization. NCMEC operates the CyberTipline, the nation's centralized reporting system for suspected child sexual exploitation, and works closely with law enforcement, tech companies, and other agencies to track and remove abusive content, including **CSAM** (child sexual abuse material).

New Aeon

A term used in occult and esoteric circles to describe a coming era of radical transformation—spiritual, cultural, and often violent. Popularized by occultist Aleister Crowley, the **New Aeon** (or **Aeon of Horus**) is viewed as a departure from the past, characterized by rebellion, self-deification, and the rejection of traditional morality.

Nexion

An **O9A** term for a cell or gateway that connects practitioners spiritually or organizationally to the larger cosmic current of their esoteric beliefs.

NGO

A nonprofit organization that operates independently of any government, typically focused on humanitarian, social, or political issues.

OnlyFans

A subscription-based online platform where creators share content directly with paying subscribers. While it hosts a variety of material, it is primarily known for adult and sexually explicit content.

Opher

In **O9A** terminology, a derogatory term for a non-initiate or outsider, especially one who is spiritually undeveloped or unwilling to embrace the group's extreme ideology.

Pig butchering

A cruel and calculated scam that combines romance fraud, psychological manipulation, and financial exploitation. Scammers—often part of organized criminal syndicates—"fatten up" their victims emotionally and financially over weeks or months, pretending to build a romantic or friendly relationship.

Points-For-Pain

764's reward system. Members gain rank by collecting and contributing increasingly graphic material. Suicide and animal torture often bring the most status.

Reddit

A massive online forum system made up of thousands of user-created **"subReddit**s." While **Reddit** hosts harmless hobby communities, it also provides a semi-anonymous space for extremist ideologies, dark humor, and underground networks.

Roblox

A popular online platform that allows users—many of them children—to create, share, and play games created by other users. While marketed as a fun and educational space, **Roblox** has also been exploited by predators, scammers, and extremist recruiters due to its chat features, user-generated content, and minimal oversight.

Sacred Violence

A belief or ritual practice in which violence is framed as divinely sanctioned, purifying, or spiritually necessary.

Session

A decentralized, anonymous messaging app that routes communication through the Oxen network, avoiding the centralized servers.

Seven-Fold Way

A step-by-step spiritual and philosophical path promoted by the **Order of Nine Angles (O9A)**, designed to transform a person into a supernatural being aligned with the group's occult and elitist ideals. The path consists of seven progressive stages that involve physical hardship, isolation, infiltration, criminal transgression, and ritualistic experiences designed to harden the initiate and sever their ties with conventional morality.

Shadow Doctrine

The unwritten operating manual of **The Com**: hide in plain sight, exploit tech platforms, and spread moral decay until collapse becomes inevitable.

Siege Culture/Atomwaffen

Accelerationist, white supremacist terrorist movements. Share overlap with Com networks in goals (chaos, collapse), propaganda, and sometimes personnel.

SIM Swapping

A method of hijacking phone numbers to access bank accounts, authentication codes, or private data. Used to exploit, extort, and fund operations.

Sithian

A term used within certain online extremist subcultures—including groups like **764**—to describe individuals who embrace the dark, destructive, and chaotic aspects of existence.

Skullz Network

A cybercriminal cell aiding **764** operations through **SIM-swapping**, crypto laundering, and cyber-infrastructure management.

Steganography

The practice of hiding secret messages or data within seemingly harmless content, such as images, audio files, or videos, is known as **steganography**. Unlike encryption, which makes data unreadable without a key, **steganography** conceals the fact that a message exists at all.

Swatting

Sending police to a victim's home under false pretenses. Used as punishment, thrill, or a control tactic by digital cults.

Telegram

A cloud-based messaging app known for its encryption, speed, and ability to host large group chats or broadcast channels. Though used globally for everything from activism to news distribution, **Telegram** has also gained a reputation as a preferred platform for extremists, criminals, and groomers due to its optional anonymity, extensive file-sharing capabilities, and limited content moderation.

Terrorgram

A **Telegram**-based media ecosystem that spreads **O9A** and Com-aligned propaganda. Known for radicalizing youth through memes, guides, and encrypted links.

The Gospel of Christ

The central message of Christianity is that Jesus Christ, the Son of God, came into the world to save sinners through His death on the cross and His resurrection from the dead. It is a message of redemption, grace, and transformation—not by human effort, but by divine mercy.

TikTok

A wildly popular short-form video platform known for dance trends, memes, and increasingly, for grooming, radicalization, and digital manipulation. With an algorithm optimized for addictive engagement, **TikTok** has become a hunting ground for predators, cult recruiters, and ideologues who exploit the platform's young user base and lack of serious content moderation.

The Base

A domestic terror group training white supremacists for real-world attacks. Suspected to provide offline support and recruitment grounds for Com-affiliated actors.

The Com

A decentralized, loosely-affiliated network of extremist groups, digital cults, and ideologues unified by a shared goal of societal collapse. Not a single organization, but a **Hydra**-like coalition of chaos agents.

The Chosen Executioners

A term referring to **764** members who, in a post-collapse world, may serve as the enforcers of the **Galactic Imperium**—a sadistic priesthood of the **Antichrist**.

The Shadow Fruit

A biblical metaphor applied to the outcome of Com-style networks: spiritual decay, societal breakdown, and the loss of innocence that often occurs in youth.

Tiwaz Division

A paramilitary offshoot of **O9A** focused on ritual murder and violent initiation. Promotes **sacred violence** as a pathway to spiritual evolution.

Tribute Payments

In online criminal circles, especially among groups like **764**, "**tribute payments**" refer to coerced or voluntary transfers of money, explicit content, or degrading acts made by victims to their abusers as a form of submission, loyalty, or humiliation.

Übermensch

A German term meaning "superman" or "overman," originally coined by philosopher Friedrich Nietzsche. The Übermensch represents an ideal person who transcends conventional morality and societal norms to create and live by his/her own values.

Unholy Vault

A black market for encrypted files containing **CSAM**, gore, and **Lorebooks**. Used to rank members and distribute content among trusted circles.

VPN (Virtual Private Network)

A technology that creates a secure, encrypted connection over the internet, allowing users to hide their location, mask their IP address, and browse anonymously. **VPNs** are commonly used for privacy protection, bypassing censorship, or accessing geo-restricted content. However, they are also frequently used by criminals and extremist groups—like those associated with **764**—to conceal their identities, evade law enforcement, and operate in the dark corners of the web without detection.

X (formerly Twitter)

A social media platform owned by Elon Musk, rebranded from **Twitter** to "**X**" in 2023. Musk envisions **X** as an "everything app" combining messaging, payments, video, and social interaction. The platform has become increasingly popular among free-speech advocates, conspiracy theorists, and extremist communities alike, including some affiliated with **764**.

www.ingramcontent.com/pod-product-compliance
Lightning Source LLC
LaVergne TN
LVHW051559080426
835510LV00020B/3053